REJOICING WITH THE PSALMIST

G. ARTHUR KEOUGH

Pacific Press Publishing Association
Boise, Idaho
Oshawa, Ontario, Canada

Edited by Bonnie Widicker
Designed by Linda Griffith Criswell
Cover photo by Betty Blue
Typeset in 10/12 Century Schoolbook

Library of Congress Cataloging in Publication Data

Keough, G. Arthur, 1909-1989
    Rejoicing with the psalmist / G. Arthur Keough.
        p. 125
    ISBN 0-8163-0897-7
    1. Bible. O.T. Psalms—Devotional literature. I. Title.
BS1430.4.K42 1990
223'.206—dc20   89-63479
                                                           CIP

90 91 92 93 94 · 5 4 3 2 1

Contents

G. Arthur Keough

1909-1989

Just weeks after completing this book, Elder G. Arthur Keough passed away in Takoma Park, Maryland, at the age of eighty. Born of missionary parents in the Middle East, Elder Keough returned to his birthplace to serve after he completed his formal education. He devoted fifty-seven years of his life to Adventist education as a teacher, principal, professor, and department chairman, twenty-seven of them in the Middle East. Under his guidance, Middle East College was founded in Beirut. Although retired, he was teaching a course at Columbia Union College at the time of his death.

Introduction

Poetry and song are two gifts that God has given us to express our deepest emotions and relationships. Since people experience a gamut of moods, they have created songs to go with those moods. Thus a mother sings a lullaby as she puts her child to sleep. The young Romeo, with thoughts of romance, sings to his Juliet, and both experience pleasure. The soldier on his way to battle finds a martial tune to lift his spirits and quicken his steps. The dirge is reserved for times of sorrow and death.

Religious experience is also enhanced by songs suitable to the season. Certain songs we sing at Christmastime, when we celebrate the birth of our Lord. At Easter we sing about the cross and the resurrection. We invoke God's presence with a hymn, and we sing a hymn to close a religious service. Our occasions of worship could be dull if they were not enlivened with congregational singing.

We have always had poets in our midst, men and women who, with special insight, plumb the depths of human experience. They do so in unforgettable words, and often set their words to music, which enhances the message. We gladly listen to the songs, and if we have the gift, we sing along. We are grateful for those who can express our inner thoughts in ways that we could not possibly match. We thank God for those who use the gifts that He has given them to His glory.

The Bible, too, has its poetry, a whole book called the Psalms. There are snatches of poetry from Genesis to Revelation, poetic outbursts from writers as they contemplate the miracles of God or the wonders of creation, or as they record

5

the singing of others in their joy. But religious poetic expression is concentrated in the Psalms. Here we find the prayers and praises of men of God, from Moses to David, from Solomon to poets in the time of the Babylonian exile. King David is undoubtedly the greatest contributor, but there are other authors, named and anonymous.

Have you noticed that the Psalms are favorite reading for all those who want to enjoy a right relationship with their God? Life is not always easy; it contains moments of joy, but also times of perplexity. There are times when we recognize the blessings of God, but sometimes we feel godforsaken. Very often we feel alone in our experience, as though no one else in the universe understands us. It is at such times that we can find comfort in knowing that men of God have felt the same way, and when we learn how they overcame their bouts of depression by expressing their confidence in God, we, too, may find our way back to a wholesome Christian experience.

Did you know that Jesus quoted from the Psalms more than from any other book? His teaching in the Sermon on the Mount is replete with principles from the Psalms. He and His disciples sang a psalm as they left the last supper to go to the Garden of Gethsemane (see Mark 14:26). And on the cross Jesus let out the cry: "My God, My God, why hast thou forsaken me?" (Psalm 22:1, KJV). A study of the book of Psalms will certainly repay itself, not only in terms of learning from men of God the way of victory over sin and a sinful environment, but also in terms of discovering what the Christian way of life involves.

What does it mean to grow spiritually with the psalmist? It means to learn from the psalmist what made him a man of God and to follow his example. It means to grow in grace and the knowledge of God (see Colossians 1:10). It means to have a heart open to the Holy Spirit, sensitive to His promptings, so that the life we live is not on the level of an unregenerated heart, but is directed by the Holy Spirit (see Romans 8:4). When we are endowed with the Spirit, we are able to help those who have fallen inadvertently into sin and need a helping hand to recover (see Galatians 6:1). What a privilege it is to be a "spiritual" person, to be an instrument of grace in a world that needs a manifestation of God's grace.

The psalmists knew what it was like to live in a wicked world where wicked designs and purposes seemed to prevail. They knew what it was like to be objects of scorn, to be at the mercy of their enemies, or so it seemed. They did not always understand their situations, but they knew that there was a God who could deliver them. Their hope was in God. They knew that their struggle was not so much with human foes, as with cosmic powers and superhuman forces of evil (see Ephesians 6:12). But they knew that their God was greater than any foe, and in their God they trusted.

Chapter 1
Singing to the Lord: Music in the Life of the Church

The psalmist exhorts us again and again to "sing to the Lord." In one psalm he says, "Shout for joy to the Lord, all the earth" (Psalm 100:1), as if to say, if you cannot sing, at least you can shout! It is not the music of the sound that matters, but the expression of an inner experience that cannot be contained.

Notice the direction of the singing; it is "to the Lord." If we are atheists, we cannot sing to the Lord because, in our opinion, there is no Lord to hear the song. If we are agnostics, we cannot sing to the Lord because we are not sure that He exists. If we are deists and convinced that God is so far away that we cannot reach Him by song or any other means, then singing to the Lord is futile. We can sing to the Lord only if, like the psalmist, we are convinced that there is a God in heaven, that He is concerned with what goes on in the earth, that He hears us when we pray to Him, and that it matters to Him whether we sing to Him.

It is true that at times we do not feel like singing. The psalmist in captivity in Babylon said: "By the rivers of Babylon we sat and wept when we remembered Zion" (Psalm 137:1). He tells us that the Jews in captivity hung their harps on the poplars because there was no use for them. When their captors asked them to sing, they said: "How can we sing the songs of the Lord while in a foreign land?" (verse 4). Although during times of deep sorrow we cannot sing, we experience many occasions when songs to the Lord can and should spring forth spontaneously from our lips.

The psalmist sets the example. He says: "I will sing of the Lord's great love forever" (Psalm 89:1). Some topics are always relevant, and the love of God is one of them. Samuel Webbe (1740-1816) expresses this thought beautifully in his hymn when he says:

New every morning is the love
Our wakening and uprising prove;
Through sleep and darkness safely brought,
Restored to life and power and thought.

We cannot cease to sing to the Lord when we think of His constant love and care.

Occasions of Singing to the Lord

The first instance the Bible records of the angelic hosts shouting for joy was when they observed the Lord lay the foundations of the earth (see Job 38:4-7). The psalmist says: "Let all the earth fear the Lord; let all the people of the world revere him. For he spoke, and it came to be; he commanded, and it stood firm" (Psalm 33:8, 9).

The prophet Isaiah puts it this way: "As the rain and the snow come down from heaven, and do not return to it without watering the earth and making it bud and flourish, so that it yields seed for the sower and bread for the eater, so is my word that goes out from my mouth: it will not return to me empty, but will accomplish what I desire and achieve the purpose for which I sent it" (Isaiah 55:10, 11).

But why did the morning stars sing together and all the angels, or sons of God, shout for joy? Was it merely because of the mystery of the great power of creation? Perhaps so, but I believe it was because they also saw the intricacies and interrelatedness of all creation, and the beauty of it all. Modern science has made tremendous progress in revealing the mysteries of nature, but every discovery has opened up new areas still to be explored. There seems to be no end to the vastness of the universe or the intricacy of detail in every particle of creation. Furthermore, the colors, the shapes, the renewing forces within nature, all make one cry out in thankfulness and praise to the One who brought everything into being. We concur with the Creator that He has made all things good, nay, very good (see Genesis 1:31).

You and I cannot see the wonders of nature without responding in some form of exclamation. William Wordsworth has said:

My heart leaps up when I behold
A rainbow in the sky:
So was it when my life began;
So is it now I am a man;
So be it when I shall grow old,
Or let me die!

How true it is that we cease to live when we cease to appreciate the wonders of creation and forget the One who is the author of it all!

The psalmist was aware of the wonders of creation, and, by extension, the Creator. He says: "The heavens declare the glory of God; the skies proclaim the work of his hands. . . . Their voice goes out into all the earth, their words to the ends of the world" (Psalm 19:1-4). It is no wonder that he felt like singing to the Lord. In fact, he urges the singing of a new song, because God has done "marvelous things" that include providing for our salvation (see Psalm 98:1, 2).

Our experience of God's providence also causes us to sing to the Lord. God's leading to victory caused Moses and the children of Israel to sing a song recorded in Exodus 15. "I will sing to the Lord, for he is highly exalted," are the first words. Miriam the prophetess and sister to Moses, "took a tambourine in her hand, and all the women followed her, with tambourines and dancing" (verse 20), and Miriam sang the introductory words that Moses had used. The children of Israel responded with singing when they saw how God had led them to safety and freedom.

Do we not respond in the same way when we are conscious

of God's leading and providing? I remember the time my father came home to inform us that the church had granted him a furlough. He had been in Egypt for ten years without a break. Now we as a family could return to England, to relatives and friends. How we jumped around and shouted! How we danced and sang! We as children had never seen England, but we thought of it as home. We had never seen our relatives, but we knew that we would be glad to see them and they us. Soon we would be packing our things and traveling by boat and train. "Hurrah," we said. "God is good to us!"

But times for singing to the Lord may also be times of apparent hardship, times when we are being persecuted for our faith. This was the case of Paul and Silas as they were in prison. We read the story in Acts 16:19-34. Somehow the two men did not murmur or complain. For them it was a privilege to suffer as their Lord had done. They raised their voices in prayer and praise, and the jailers listened with great surprise. The jailers could not understand how people in pain could sing songs of joy. They were more used to groans and curses, and shrieks arising from discomfort. But they also did not know why Paul and Silas could be happy in the most discouraging circumstances.

Then came the earthquake that opened all the doors and loosened all the chains of the prisoners. The chief jailer awakened from his sleep and, seeing the situation, thought first of taking his life. But Paul encouraged him not to do so, and the final result was that the jailer's family "was filled with joy, because they had come to believe in God" (verse 34). Here we see the tremendous power and witness of singing to the Lord.

The Injunction to Sing

With Paul's background of experience in singing, it is no wonder that he, writing to the Ephesians and the Colossians, exhorts them to "speak to one another with psalms, hymns, and spiritual songs. Sing and make music in your heart to the Lord, always giving thanks to God the Father for everything, in the name of our Lord Jesus Christ" (Ephesians 5:19, 20; see also Colossians 3:16). He knew the effect of a song on himself and on others. He knew that hymn singing could change a mood, could give a testimony of faith, could build up one's confidence in God, could give one courage to continue to do what is right, regardless of adverse circumstances.

From this exhortation to sing, William Barclay draws the conclusion that the early church was a singing church (*Letters to the Galatians and the Ephesians*, p. 197). It had its songs and hymns, but it also used the psalms, and from the psalms it would be encouraged to sing to the Lord. There would be singing, not only in the church, but also in the home, at the workplace, and wherever it seemed possible and appropriate.

Paul is not the only one to encourage singing. James says: "Is any one of you in trouble? He should pray. Is anyone happy? Let him sing songs of praise" (James 5:13).

Sacred songs are to be clear in their meaning. It is not sufficient that the tunes should be catchy and forceful. The words must also be clearly understood. Paul writes to the Corinthians: "I will pray with my spirit, but I will also pray with my mind. I will sing with my spirit, but I will also sing with my mind" (1 Corinthians 14:15). All singing must proceed from a thoughtful mind and a willing, devoted spirit. It must appeal to the mind as well as to the ear and the heart. There is nothing frivolous in singing a hymn, and no frivolity should ever characterize any part of the church service.

The Value of Singing to the Lord

Obviously singing to the Lord has much value to the person and to the community at large. It expresses joy in times of happiness and gratitude in times of stress.

A glance at the church hymnal will reveal the many occasions when singing is appropriate. There are hymns for the morning and hymns for eventide; hymns to open worship and hymns to bring it to a satisfactory close; hymns that express gratitude to God and hymns that commemorate various events in the life of Christ; hymns of repentance, hymns of consecration, and hymns of praise.

One danger in hymn singing is that we limit ourselves to a

favorite few. We need to expand our repertoire, so that our worship may become more meaningful to us. We need to be better acquainted with the church hymnal and the psalms.

Mrs. White has said: "Music forms a part of God's worship in the courts above, and we should endeavor, in our songs of praise, to approach as nearly as possible to the harmony of the heavenly choirs. Singing, as a part of religious service, is as much an act of worship as is prayer. The heart must feel the spirit of the song to give it right expression" (*Patriarchs and Prophets*, p. 594).

The psalmist refers to the use of musical instruments in connection with singing. He says: "Praise the Lord with the harp; make music to him on the ten-stringed lyre. . . . Play skillfully, and shout for joy" (Psalm 33:2, 3).

The use of musical instruments enhances the song. Psalm 81 says: "Begin the music, strike the tambourine, play the melodious harp and lyre. Sound the ram's horn" (verses 2, 3). Obviously there is a proper use for those musical instruments as a part of worship. It's interesting that the psalms have received their name from a musical instrument with strings that could be plucked. David knew how to play several instruments, and, doubtless, in this way was able to appreciate the value of music to the soul.

The Psalms as Songs We Can Sing

The psalms have been sung for centuries, first by the Jews and later by the early Christians. Many have been modernized for our use today. A glance at a hymnbook will reveal that more hymns contain allusions to the book of Psalms than to any other book in the Bible. Psalm 23 is a favorite, but other psalms are referred to in whole or in part.

We know that Jesus and His disciples sang a hymn at the close of their last supper together (see Matthew 26:30). They sang Psalm 113 and Psalm 116, both psalms expressing trust in and praise to God. God is good in providing all our needs. Even though there are times of anguish, the psalmist can say: "Be at rest once more, O my soul, for the Lord has been good to you" (Psalm 116:7).

Mrs. White has said: "With a song, Jesus in His earthly life met temptation. Often when sharp, stinging words were spoken, often when the atmosphere about Him was heavy with gloom, with dissatisfaction, distrust, or oppressive fear, was heard His song of faith and holy cheer" (*Education*, p. 166).

Here is another picture of Jesus: "While Christ was working at the carpenter's bench, others would sometimes surround Him trying to cause Him to be impatient; but He would begin singing some of the beautiful psalms, and before they realized what they were doing, they had joined with Him in singing, influenced, as it were, by the power of the Holy Spirit which was there" (*The Adventist Home*, p. 443).

There are good reasons that the psalms have been so popular in religious life. They were composed for the priests and used in the sanctuary services. But, more important, they deal with the wide range of religious experience. Here is a beautiful description of the topics they cover:

> The psalms of David pass through the whole range of experience, from the depths of conscious guilt and self-condemnation to the loftiest faith and the most exalted communing with God. His life record declares that sin can bring only shame and woe, but that God's love and mercy can reach to the deepest depths, that faith will lift up the repenting soul to share the adoption of the sons of God. Of all the assurances His word contains, it is one of the strongest testimonies to the faithfulness, the justice, and the covenant mercy of God (*Patriarchs and Prophets*, p. 754).

It is no wonder, therefore, that the psalms have been so popular, both in ancient and modern times, with those whose hearts reach out for a solution to sin and find it in the God of Abraham, Isaac, and Jacob.

What a blessing it is to know that God is our Shepherd, that He cares for us as a good shepherd cares for his sheep. What a relief to know that God is our fortress and strength, a very present help in times of trouble. How fortunate we are to have a God who communicates His will, who forgives our transgressions, and who restores us to full fellowship with Himself. Surely we find the psalms hymns that we can sing, and sing to God's glory.

Singing as a Part of Worship

"The melody of praise is the atmosphere of heaven." It is not surprising, therefore, if those whose hearts are in tune with heaven find themselves bursting into song. "Heaven's communion begins on earth. We learn here the key note of its praise" (*Education*, pp. 161, 168).

On the Sabbath it is our privilege to meet with fellow members in the church and to raise our voices in songs of praise and commitment. Each one of us is uplifted spiritually in the process, and we are being prepared to join the angelic hosts in their singing in heaven.

The ability to sing is a gift from God that we should use only to His glory. Unfortunately, some use the talent for self-gratification. God forbid that this should be so among Christians. Since God is worshiped with song and music in the heavens above, it is only natural that we should raise our voices in praise to Him while we are here on earth. We come before Him with "thanksgiving and the sound of singing" (Isaiah 51:3). As we do so, we bring honor to His name, and He, in turn, reveals to us His wonderful plan of salvation (see Psalm 50:23).

Singing in the church service is as important as prayer and the preaching of the Word. By it we are drawn closer to one another and to God. Music has a powerful influence on our lives. How often, as we go about our daily duties, a tune will come to our minds, and with the tune the words. Since our minds can focus on only one topic at a time, while we are singing words of praise to God we cannot be thinking critical or discouraging thoughts.

Singing is a part of church worship in which we can all take an active part. We stand up to sing. We raise our voices with others and sing in harmony. We affirm our faith, we proclaim our love, we express our longings, and we offer our prayers in words that we find more beautiful and meaningful than any words that we could compose ourselves. Thank God for the godly poets. Thank God for the godly musicians who have prepared our hymnbooks. Thank God for those talented people in the church who can play the organ and other instruments of music to our delight and to God's glory. Our church services would lack much beauty and inspiration without the singing and the accompaniment of musical instruments.

There will be joyous singing in the earth made new. Adam will be there. He will rejoice as he is reinstated in his first dominion. Here is a picture that has been presented to us:

> Transported with joy, he beholds the trees that were once his delight—the very trees whose fruit he himself had gathered in the days of his innocence and joy. He sees the vines that his own hands have trained, the very flowers that he once loved to care for. His mind grasps the reality of the scene; he comprehends that this is indeed Eden restored, more lovely now than when he was banished from it. The Saviour leads him to the tree of life and plucks the glorious fruit and bids him eat. He looks about him and beholds a multitude of his family redeemed, standing in the Paradise of God. Then he casts his glittering crown at the feet of Jesus and, falling upon His breast, embraces the Redeemer. He touches the golden harp, and the vaults of heaven echo the triumphant song: "Worthy, worthy, worthy is the Lamb that was slain, and lives again!" The family of Adam take up the strain and cast their crowns at the Saviour's feet as they bow before Him in adoration (*The Great Controversy*, p. 648).

May our singing today be a preparation for that great event, through Jesus Christ our Lord.

Chapter 2
The Road to Lasting Joy

Psalm 1

When Moses came to the end of his career with the children of Israel in the wilderness, he summoned the people and challenged them with these words: "See, I have set before you today life and prosperity, death and destruction." "Choose life, so that you and your children may live" (Deuteronomy 30:15, 19).

Likewise Joshua, after he had successfully led the children of Israel into the Promised Land, urged the people gathered together to choose whom they would serve and indicated that he and his family would serve the Lord (see Joshua 24:15).

Jesus, too, pointed out that two roads stretched out before every individual, one leading to life and the other leading to destruction. He urged His hearers to enter the narrow gate and walk the narrow road "that leads to life" (see Matthew 7:13, 14).

In the first psalm we find the same spirit, an indication of two roads, one leading to life and prosperity and the other leading to annihilation. It is up to us to decide which road we want to take.

The first psalm has been described as a wisdom psalm. It reads very much like the book of Proverbs, telling us the right things to do and the results of doing what is wrong. The wise man has said: "Wisdom is supreme; therefore get wisdom. Though it cost all you have, get understanding" (Proverbs 4:7).

Scholars have noted the suitability of this psalm as an introduction to the book of Psalms. It lays down the basic principles of life, a theme that will be taken up and expanded in the other 149 psalms. You and I need to be directed in the way that we should go, and, therefore, we approach the study of the psalms with anticipation.

The first word is *blessed*. The Hebrew the word *ashre* can be translated into several English words. Hence the Amplified Bible gives: "happy, fortunate, prosperous and enviable." The New English Bible, the Good News Bible, and the Jewish Publication Society's English version of the Scriptures, all translate the word as "happy." *Ashre* is a deep-seated joy, a joy that is not affected by immediate circumstances.

We catch something of the meaning of *ashre*-blessedness when we read the Beatitudes. There Jesus is obviously referring to the blessedness spoken of by the psalmist, when he says: "Blessed are those who mourn." He is not referring to immediate circumstances. He refers to another aspect of mourning; "they will be comforted" (Matthew 5:4). There is a wholeness of experience that is denoted by blessedness. The immediate situation may not be pleasant or happy, but the end result is satisfaction. In other words, the happiness spoken of by the psalmist is so deep-seated that it is not affected by temporary pain or hardship; it is a relationship with God that brings favor and satisfaction, for all true happiness, all blessedness, comes primarily from God.

"*Blessed is the man*" (verse 1). At first glance we might want to change the word *man* to *person* so as to include both male and female. But A. A. Anderson says: "This formula is not addressed to men in general but to that kind of person who is described in verses 1-3. Women and children are included because, in the Israelite view, part of man's true happiness is his family—a good wife and many children—and so *his* blessings (as well as his responsibilities) are shared by the whole family" (*The New Century Bible Commentary, Psalms 1-72*, p. 58). Thus men, women, and children can share in the blessedness spoken of by the psalmist.

The Wrong Road: Conduct to Avoid

Following one of the principles of Hebrew poetry, the

psalmist proceeds in verse 1 to give us three more or less parallel statements:

"who does not walk in the counsel of the wicked"
"or stand in the way of sinners"
"or sit in the scat of the mockers."

Although we recognize the parallelism, we cannot miss a progression of thought in the verbs: walking, standing, and last, sitting.

The psalmist also lists three kinds of people: The wicked or ungodly; the sinners or those who transgress God's law; the mockers or the scornful. Notice the progression of activity:

1. First, we listen to people around us, regardless of their relationship to God. Perhaps they are our peers. We pay more attention to what they have to say than to what our parents say. We want to be part of the crowd because we consider ourselves part of the new generation. We do not want to be singled out as different. Furthermore, some standards may seem to be old-fashioned. The group we are with does not deny the existence of God, but it ignores God. It is worldly wise and follows the fashions of the day. We find it easier to go along with them, and so we "walk" with them, following their advice in most of the decisions of life.

2. Second, we stand with sinners who definitely transgress God's commands. Generally, they seem to prosper. Their motto is, Do what meets with success. Even though they know what is right and what is wrong, they do what seems to suit their own interests best. We "stand" with them because we enjoy their company, and although we have twinges of conscience sometimes, we quiet our conscience by saying that we are doing quite well and have nothing to worry about. Thus, in time, we have no guilty conscience. Although the truth may be presented to us, we brush it aside as irrelevant.

3. The third and final step taken by those who are determined to go the wrong way is to sit in judgment on the right doers. Thus they become "mockers" or the scornful. They feel

that their course of behavior is the right course for them, and although they are willing to concede that there may be other courses to take, they are sorry for those who are so duped as not to follow their own way of living. They openly deride those who keep the commandments of God. Usually they are deaf to any appeals to do what is right.

In his *Psalms: Studies on Book One,* H. A. Ironside has noted that the verbs used in the first verse of the psalm are all in the perfect tense. He would therefore translate the verse this way: "Blessed is the man who hath not walked . . . nor stood . . . nor sat. . . ." He concludes: "He is not expressing the blessedness of a man who was once a sinner and has been turned to righteousness and no longer walks in the counsel of the ungodly, nor stands in the way of sinners, nor sits in the seat of the scornful. But he is telling us of the blessedness of the Man who has never done any of these things, the Man who never took his own way, the Man who never walked with the world as part of it, who never did a thing in opposition to the will of God" (page 9).

He goes on to point out that even the Jews will agree that this passage cannot apply to Abraham, since he made mistakes; nor to Moses, who also had his faults. It can only apply to Jesus Christ. Jesus then is the supreme example of what to avoid and what we may rightly do in order to inherit the kingdom. Psalm 1, like Psalm 22 and some other psalms, is, therefore, predictive and normative.

The Right Road: Meditating on the Word of God

"But his delight" (verse 2). The second verse of this psalm begins with a strong adversative—*but.* We turn away from the negative to the positive. The negative is always clear and forceful. Eight of the Ten Commandments are negative and tell us clearly what we should not do. Two commandments are positive: the fourth commandment, telling us to remember the Sabbath day to keep it holy; and the fifth commandment, reminding us to honor our parents. We need both kinds of commandments, the ones that tell us what *not* to do, and those that tell us what we *ought* to do.

It was so in the Garden of Eden. Our first parents were told what they might eat, and they were also told what they might not eat. In this way they could exercise their power of choice and indicate which side of the controversy between Christ and Satan they were on.

What, then, is the emphasis of the life that is dedicated to God? It is one of pleasure and delight. For instance, every Sabbath is called a delight, and there is joy in the Lord (see Isaiah 58:13, 14).

The psalmist is specific: "His delight is in the law of the Lord." The man and woman of God will not only find the law of the Lord interesting and valuable, but will find the law a delight to dwell upon. This means that Bible study will be an experience to be enjoyed, not merely a duty to be performed. This experience is not a transitory delight, a passing phase of excitement; it is the experience of always joyfully anticipating the study of God's Word. It is a recognition that nothing is more valuable to us than knowing God's will. The more we know about God and His plans for us, the more we are delighted and the more we want to learn.

Perhaps the word *delight* is a kind of measurement that lets us know how much we appreciate the privilege of having and studying God's Word. To "delight in" is more than to have a "desire for." Paul had a desire to keep the law. He recognized that it was good. But he found that he could not keep it (see Romans 7:14-19). It was only when he found salvation in Jesus Christ that he found the way to delight in the law. It is the same with you and me. It is only when we know the saving grace of God in our lives that we can truly delight in God's Word.

The Hebrew word for *law* here is *torah*. It includes more than the Ten Commandments. It includes all the teachings of the Pentateuch, and, by extension, the Old Testament. In the Scriptures we read not only of God's prescriptive laws, but we also learn about His character, His *hesed* or loving-kindness, His fidelity to His covenant promises, and His plan for our salvation. We also see how long-suffering He is with us as sinners. He is not willing that any should perish.

The psalmist refers to God as JAHWEH, the God who revealed Himself to Moses in the burning bush as the I AM (see Exodus 3:14). He is the one and only God (see Deuteronomy 6:4). He is the ever-present, ever-living God, the One who has acted in history from the very beginning, and who is working out His purposes to the very end. He is your God and mine, ever active in our lives and seeking our salvation. If we recognize what all this means to us, then we shall always find His law and His teaching a delight.

"*On his law he meditates.*" The Hebrew word for *meditates* is the word used in the second psalm for "plot" (see Psalm 2:1). It is a strong word suggesting "reciting" and "uttering." Perhaps we have a picture here of a person reading the Word of God aloud. He is making sure that he reads it correctly, that he understands every word and appreciates its full meaning. He is not satisfied with half measures. In this way the Word of God becomes a part of him.

There is always the danger that we gloss over the words of Scripture, that we miss out on the message that it contains for us, both personally and collectively. It is very easy to be so familiar with passages of Scripture that we gloss over the meaning. In this connection it can be very valuable to have several versions at hand so that we can compare the one with the other, and thus find a meaning that might otherwise be missed.

"*Day and night.*" These words indicate that our study of the Bible should be on a continual basis. When we remember that we are living in a world of spiritual darkness, we realize the importance of having the Bible as a lamp to our feet and a light to our pathway (see Psalm 119:105). We need it in every circumstance of life.

Once again we have a principle whereby we can gauge our Christian commitment to God's Word. Are we as faithful to it as we ought to be? What is it that keeps us away from Bible study? Are we too satisfied with our present knowledge? Are we too busy in the matter of earning a living that we are remiss in studying the principles of our salvation?

Interestingly enough, we have a much larger body of Scripture than that possessed by the psalmist. He may have had the Pentateuch and the book of Job and perhaps some of the contemporary writings of the prophets. We have sixty-six books full of poetry and prose, prophecy and exhortation, letters and the life of Jesus. We have a rich heritage that we should never neglect.

We are in constant danger, not so much that the Bible will be taken away from us, but that we will be dragged away from the Bible. Furthermore, the time will come when there will be a famine of the Word of God, and unless we have made adequate preparation by careful study of the truths revealed in the Bible, we may find ourselves slipping away from our religious foundations.

A young man I knew in the Middle East used to learn large portions of the Bible by memory. He was an enthusiastic witness for Christ and used to talk to his fellow soldiers about the truths in the Bible. One day an officer became annoyed with the young man and confiscated the Bible. Did that make any difference to the witness? Not at all! He continued to preach at every opportunity that came his way and recited Scripture instead of reading it. He said to me, "They took the Bible away from me, but they could not take away the Bible in my heart."

The Fruitful Life

"He is like a tree planted by streams of water" (verse 3). The apt simile of a tree and a man's life is used a number of times in Scripture. Thus the psalmist speaks of the righteous as flourishing "like a palm tree, they will grow like a cedar of Lebanon" (Psalm 92:12). The palm tree provides a wide variety of dates, and the cedar is a symbol of strength and longevity. Cedar wood was used for the building of the temple. Jeremiah says that the man who trusts in God "will be like a tree planted by the water that sends out its roots by the stream. It does not fear when heat comes; its leaves are always green. It has no worries in a year of drought and never fails to bear fruit" (Jeremiah 17:7, 8). The picture is almost the same as the one in our psalm. Isaiah speaks of people who will be called "oaks of righteousness" (Isaiah 61:3).

Nebuchadnezzar had a dream in which he saw himself as a tree "in the middle of the land. Its height was enormous. The tree grew large and strong and its top touched the sky; it was visible to the ends of the earth. Its leaves were beautiful, its fruit abundant, and on it was food for all. Under it the beasts of the field found shelter, and the birds of the air lived in its branches" (Daniel 4:10-12). But the tree came to a sad end. Daniel's interpretation was fulfilled to the letter, and the king came to realize that his pride meant his fall, and his recognition of God as supreme meant his restoration (see verses 13-37).

Jesus made a significant statement regarding plants. He said, "Every plant that my heavenly Father has not planted will be pulled up by the roots" (Matthew 15:13). It is God who decides what will live and what will not (see Ezekiel 17:5-9, 22-24). It is our relationship to God that determines whether we shall live or die, whether we are fruitful or pulled up. It is well that we recognize our total dependence on God for everything. The blessing is that He is gracious. He plants and transplants us; He places us where we can get all the water and nourishment we need; He causes us to be fruitful and a blessing to others. We have no need to fear drought or danger, for He protects us.

"*Whatever he does prospers*." The psalmist seems to have forgotten his simile here! He sees the godly man strong, stable, fruitful, and happy. Now he sees him prospering in everything to which he sets his hand. It is taken for granted, of course, that everything he sets out to do is according to God's will. Here we have the picture of a man as God intended he should live, enjoying his existence, free to choose, but always making the right choices and maintaining a right relationship with his God. Can one choose for oneself anything better?

What the Wicked Are Like

"*Not so the wicked! They are like chaff that the wind blows away*" (verse 4). The scene is a threshing floor in the Middle East. The wheat has been harvested. It lies on the threshing floor, a mixture of grain and chaff or husks. The season provides a suitable wind, and the winnowing begins. People with forks throw the mixture into the air. The chaff is blown away, and the heavier grain falls to the threshing floor. It is hard work, but eventually the farmer has a pile of grain separated from the chaff. This grain will be used for feeding the family.

Chaff! The very sound of the word suggests something comparatively worthless. Blown away by the wind! There is nothing stable about chaff. The image suggests that the wicked are unstable in their actions, undependable in their lives, uncertain in their reactions, of no worth except as God can make use of them for His own purposes (consider, for example, the pharaoh of Egypt at the time of the Exodus). They have chosen not to listen to God; they have decided to go their own selfish way, and now they are lost.

What do the wicked have to present in defense of their wickedness? Nothing! They have had every opportunity to repent, to turn away from their wicked ways, but they have spurned every offer of mercy. They know they are guilty and can only expect retribution. What a prospect!

"Therefore the wicked will not stand in the judgment" (verse 5). We might restate it in an English idiom: they have no leg to stand on! They have no excuse! They can only blame themselves for the situation they are in. Can you imagine the remorse that every one of them must feel in the circumstances? They can expect only one future—total annihilation.

"Nor sinners in the assembly of the righteous." The wicked cannot be comfortable in a place of worship, where the righteous are assembled. They feel condemned. Therefore, in a sense, it is better for them to be annihilated. They would never be happy in heaven.

Their annihilation is not a work that God is anxious to do. It is sad to see someone who has been created in the image of God bring himself or herself to the place where separation from God and His bounties is the only solution. It is God's strange act to destroy the wicked, and when the event takes place in the presence of the holy angels and the Lamb (see

Revelation 14:10), there will be silence in heaven. No harp will be heard on that occasion, no angelic choir will sing. But when the universe is cleansed from all sin, there will be a sigh of relief, a turning away from a sorry past to a glorious future. And to God will be the glory forever and ever.

Conclusion

"For the Lord watches over the way of the righteous" (verse 6). It is the Lord's doing from beginning to end. He has communicated with us. He has made provision for our salvation. He has revealed His love and constancy. He has helped us make the right decisions. He has given us the power to overcome evil. He has forgiven us when we have failed and asked for His forgiveness. He has been marvelously patient with us. He has provided our every need. We can only thank and praise Him. He watches over us as a hen watches over her chicks and seeks to bring them under the protection of her wings. What more can we ask? The least that we can do is to thank and praise Him and always seek to do His will and accomplish His purposes for us.

"But the way of the wicked will perish." What a blessing it is to know that there will be a finality to wickedness! We may be sorry for sinners when there is hope for their salvation, but we may be sure that God will not destroy them until they have so thoroughly associated themselves with sin that no distinction can be made between sin and sinner.

Our God is a God of infinite love and kindness, but He is also a God of justice. When Abraham expressed the rhetorical question, "Will not the Judge of all the earth do right?" (Genesis 18:25), he was expressing an eternal truth. God is long-suffering and gracious, but there comes a time when justice must express itself in condemnation and annihilation of all the forces of evil. When God's name is vindicated, there can be only one outcome, the triumph of truth and righteousness and the end of all wickedness.

Chapter 3
God's Sovereignty: How Foolish to Resist!
Psalm 2

Have you ever wondered why some people persist in using tobacco when they know it is injurious to their health? Does it surprise you that companies continue to produce and sell alcoholic beverages when the harmful effects of alcoholism are well documented? Because of sin, human nature contains a perverse streak that makes it difficult for some people to follow reason and pushes them to act selfishly and greedily.

The psalmist has his own query and surprise. Why, O why, he asks, do the nations rage and the people engage in foolish activities?

Opposing God: A Mark of Foolishness (verses 1-3)

The psalmist sees kings and rulers gathering together against the Lord. He is surprised because the Lord, or Yahweh, is the only true God and sovereign of the universe. How can anyone in his right mind—least of all kings and princes, who are expected to be wiser than others—even imagine they can oppose God?

For one thing there is the contrast of power. Can a flea say to an elephant, "You stop in your tracks!" and expect to be obeyed? Will the elephant pay any attention? Surely the created must realize how puny he is in comparison with the Creator. Surely those in authority must know that their power is limited, not only with men, but certainly with God.

Second, God's goodness and love—manifest in the creation

29

of our planet, in His dealings with our first parents, and in the salvation that He wrought for the children of Israel—should convince thoughtful people that going contrary to God is to fight against their best interests.

Furthermore, human rage or anger has never accomplished any good thing. Have you seen a boy lose his temper? Have you seen him stamp his foot, fling his arms, and cause damage? I knew a young man who was so disgusted with the service he was getting from a college cafeteria that he threw a trayful of dishes on the ground and broke them. He may have been expressing his inner feelings, but no change in the service resulted. I asked him later why he broke the dishes. He said that he had lost his temper, a trait he claimed to have inherited from his father and mother. There are some things that we inherit, but if they achieve no real good in our lives, we may as well discard them.

The kings that the psalmist refers to were not only rebelling against God, they were also opposing His *"Anointed One."* In other words, they were objecting to God's order. What was the matter with the order? They felt bound by chains and fetters.

Have you felt restricted by God's commandments? Do you feel morally bound by regulations that you wish you could get rid of? The fact is that it is only by conforming to the rules of society that we can live in freedom. Rules are not made to restrict activity, but to guide it into worthwhile channels. James calls the law of God in Scripture the "royal law" and "the perfect law that gives freedom" (James 2:8; 1:25). God's measures are not restrictive; they are enlarging, allowing for greater freedom.

What many fail to realize is that freedom comes from obedience, not from license, from submitting to a benevolent organization, not from kicking the traces. Service to God is perfect freedom, and accepting one's station in life according to God's ordinance is the best way to fulfill one's destiny.

Who is the "Anointed One"? David was anointed king (see 1 Samuel 16:13; 2 Samuel 2:4; 23:1). So were other kings. God has always shown an interest in the welfare of the people by setting up kings and putting down those who failed to lead the people aright. However, the New Testament points to Jesus as the supreme Anointed One.

In the book of Acts we read how the Christian believers, after the release of Peter and John, knelt and prayed and quoted this second psalm and applied David's words to their own situation. They said: "Indeed Herod and Pontius Pilate met together with the Gentiles and the people of Israel in this city to conspire against your holy servant Jesus, whom you anointed" (Acts 4:27; see also verses 23-26).

We know that today many do not recognize the full deity and authority of Christ. They deny the incarnation, the crucifixion, and the resurrection of our Lord. We have much for which to be thankful, if, through parents or evangelists or others, we have come to know and accept Jesus as He truly is.

Did David realize the full import of his words? It is possible that he did not. Yet writing under inspiration, he wrote better than he knew. Peter refers to prophets as not always understanding everything that had been revealed to them: "It was revealed to them that they were not serving themselves but you, when they spoke of the things that have now been told you by those who have preached the gospel to you by the Holy Spirit sent from heaven." Then he adds: "Even angels long to look into these things!" (1 Peter 1:12).

God's Response: Derision and Anger

It comes as a surprise to most of us that God, looking down on a case of rebellion, should laugh. What kind of laughter is this?

When I was young, I was taught that I should never laugh at people. I could laugh *with* them, but not *at* them. To laugh at a person is to assume a position of superiority, and this is not a position I can take. We sometimes laugh at people when we are conscious of their weaknesses and faults; this kind of laughter tends to demean. To laugh with people is to enjoy fellowship. This kind of laughter promotes camaraderie and unity.

It would not be consistent with God's character of love to

laugh at people. Yet there is always something humorous about incongruity. In this instance, God's laughter is a laughter of seeing things as they really are. How ridiculous for puny man to oppose Him.

God's response, however, is not merely laughter. He takes action to remedy the situation. The psalmist says God speaks to these rebels who do not realize what they are doing. He shows them how ridiculous their stance is. This is the "scoffing." Then He *"rebukes them in his anger"* (verse 5). When God rebukes, He convinces of wrong. He shows where people are making mistakes. The Bible as the Word of God does this very thing (see 2 Timothy 3:16). It shows us where we go astray.

The point of rebuke is to bring us to repentance, and when we repent, God places our feet on the path of righteousness. Unfortunately, there are those who refuse to repent, who are of the same mind still, no matter what evidence is placed before them. They have only judgment to look forward to.

The psalmist says that God rebukes in anger. This may come as a surprise to those of us who think of God as a God of love. How can God be angry? The fact is that God's anger is a measure of His love. When God sees a person whom He loves fall because of the machinations of a tempter, He is angry.

Do we not respond in a similar way? When we see a child offered drugs, are we not angry at those forces that bring about evil?

God terrifies in His wrath. If reason does not shake us, perhaps fear will. By all proper means God seeks to show us where we go wrong, and then He brings us back, if we are willing, to a right relationship with Himself. For this we may be truly thankful.

God Works Out His Gracious Plan

"I have installed my King on Zion, my holy hill" (verse 6). People may not always see that God's way is best. Sometimes they rebel and object. But God still pursues His plans and purposes, for they are best for all concerned. For this characteristic we may be truly thankful.

God says He has installed a king. Some commentators

think that this is a reference to an earthly king, such as King David.

It is true that God is concerned that His people be led aright. When the children of Israel wanted a king to rule over them, it was God who chose Saul and gave him a new heart for his responsibilities (see 1 Samuel 10:9). Unfortunately, Saul did not live up to his responsibilities, and God rejected him. God then chose David, the son of Jesse.

We may be sure that God has always been interested in the social order. He is anxious that leaders be qualified to lead. Thus it is that Daniel could say: "He sets up kings and deposes them" (Daniel 2:21). We may not always see God's guiding hand in history, but we may be sure that it is there.

Some scholars feel that this psalm is Messianic. God has installed a special king. Thus the NIV capitalizes the letter *K*. And thus we may see in God's statement a reference to Jesus, the Messiah.

The Magi who came to Jerusalem in the days of Herod looked for one who was to be born "king of the Jews" (Matthew 2:2). When Pilate asked Jesus, "Are you the king of the Jews?" Jesus replied, "Yes, it is as you say" (Matthew 27:11; Mark 15:2; Luke 23:3).

Of course, we recognize that the kingdom Jesus came to establish is not a kingdom of this world; it is a kingdom of those who recognize His authority. It is a kingdom that is "near" (Mark 1:15; Matthew 3:2), "within" or "among" (Luke 17:21), and still future (Revelation 12:10; 19:6-9).

With this Messianic interpretation of the psalm we can see that God has set up a King and a Saviour. In His great love for fallen humanity He sent His Son so that you and I may not perish, but have everlasting life (see John 3:16). What a gracious God is ours! Are we not truly thankful?

Jesus Himself recognized that He came to do His Father's will. On one occasion He said: "I tell you the truth, the Son can do nothing by himself; he can do only what he sees his Father doing, because whatever the Father does the Son also does" (John 5:19).

Thus God's gracious plan for man is that he be saved in the

kingdom. For this purpose He proclaimed the decree and said: *"You are my Son; today I have become your Father"* (verse 7). The capitalization of the word *Son* is another indication that scholars recognize the Messianic implication of the psalm.

A further implication exists in the acknowledgment that the Father has a Son. Do we have here a hint in the Old Testament of a Triune God? If so, we see the unity of Scripture and the unfathomable mystery of the Godhead. The apostle Paul complements this understanding when he says, "God was reconciling the world to himself in Christ" (2 Corinthians 5:19).

The psalmist goes on to show God's ultimate purpose: The Son will inherit all that man lost in the fall: (1) the loss of life through sin, and (2) the loss of dominion over the earth.

Ever since the Fall, Satan has claimed to be the prince of this world, and we must admit that those who do what is wrong are children of the devil (see John 8:44). But God has always challenged Satan's claim. In the book of Job we read that, one day, Satan presented himself before the Lord with other angelic princes. The Lord said, " 'Where have you come from?' Satan answered the Lord, 'From roaming through the earth and going back and forth in it.' " God pointed out that so long as there was a Job, one righteous person, Satan did not have complete dominion (see Job 1:6-8).

In view of God's ultimate plan, we have very good reason to sing:

Jesus shall reign wher'er the sun
Does its successive journey run;
His kingdom stretch from shore to shore,
Till moons shall wax and wane no more.—Isaac Watts.

The psalmist goes on to say: *"You will rule them with an iron scepter; you will dash them to pieces like pottery* (verse 9). What does he mean?

The imagery does not seem to coincide with the concept of a loving God and Jesus as the good shepherd. But we must remember that love and mercy do not rule out justice. God's love is infinite, but when people reject God's love and choose to be destroyed rather than to live, then God's justice is inexorable. They feel the scepter of iron; they are dashed to pieces like a potter's vessel.

What a blessing it is that we have been duly warned! In the time of judgment, if we persist in wrongdoing, we will bow down and admit that we are receiving the consequences of our choices. But why accept such a destiny, when God has done so much for our salvation?

A Piece of Good Advice

"Therefore, you kings, be wise." James says: "If any of you lacks wisdom, he should ask God, who gives generously to all without finding fault, and it will be given to him" (James 1:5). God is not only the source of authority, the one who lays down plans and carries them out; He is the one who gives us wisdom when we ask for it, generously and without finding fault.

Facts are facts and cannot be denied. Principles are principles and cannot be ignored or broken with impunity. Thank God we have the Bible that informs us of facts and principles (see Psalm 119:105). Thank God for parents and teachers who guide our footsteps. Thank God for spouses and friends who cheer us on our way. Thank God for the promise that Jesus will be with us to the end of the age (see Matthew 28:20). We are not left in darkness, for every facility is given for us to be wise unto salvation.

Your duty and mine, then, is made abundantly clear by the psalmist: "Serve the Lord with fear." What kind of fear is this? It is not the fear that we equate with terror; it is the fear that arises from love and appreciation. It is the fear lest we hurt the one we love, lest we do anything that will displease him or her. It is a fear that arises out of respect, and, in the case of God, out of awe.

What does it mean to serve the Lord? It means to do His will in every aspect of our lives. It means to do what is right even in difficult circumstances. It means to be like Daniel, who prayed even when he knew that he was breaking a law of the Medes and Persians that could not be set aside. He was not afraid of a den of lions, because he knew that God was with him.

Service with God is not slavery. It brings joy and satisfaction in this life, as well as an eternal reward in the life to come. It is therefore not surprising that the psalmist says, "*Rejoice*" (verse 11). But why does he add, "*with trembling*"?

Perhaps the thought behind the expression is to remind us that we are still human and may make mistakes. We need always to be on the alert that we do not err in any phase of our conduct. The Christian is still in a world of conflict. He needs to put on the whole armor of God (see Ephesians 6:10-18). His fight is not with mortals only. He faces "spiritual forces of evil in the heavenly realms" (verse 12). He proceeds with caution, rejoicing in the victory that can be his through Jesus Christ, but trembling lest at any moment he fail.

Thank God we can always find grace to help in time of need (see Hebrews 4:16). Thank God we can approach the throne of grace with confidence. But we must never forget our dependence upon God, and thus we rejoice with trembling.

The psalmist goes on to say: "*Kiss the Son*" (verse 12). What does he mean by this? The English version of the Jewish Publication Society of America translates: "Do homage in purity." A kiss given to a person of authority is a symbol of fealty and allegiance. It may be done in good faith, or it may be simply ceremonial.

Kissing the Son must mean acknowledging Jesus as our Lord and Saviour, and the psalmist points out that not doing so can result in a terrible fate. Do we recognize the importance of our relationship to God in Jesus Christ? It can mean a wonderful future or a miserable end. The Scripture contains nothing that we can ignore. Thank God for His revelation and His love.

The Blessedness of Trust

"*Blessed are all who take refuge in him*" (verse 12). The psalm ends with a description of those who are blessed, those who have God's approval, those who are happy and joyous. They are the ones who take refuge in God.

They live in a world that is full of danger and conflict, but they find protection in their God. They find that God is trustworthy, and they can leave their affairs in His hands with the utmost confidence.

Insurance policies do not cover every contingency. Locked doors do not always keep out robbers. Armies cannot always protect us from our enemies. But God is an all-sufficient refuge and strength, an ever present help in time of trouble.

Chapter 4
A Psalm of Praise: How Great Thou Art!

Psalm 8

This psalm is attributed to David. It reminds one of the time that King David wrote a psalm of thanksgiving to God because the ark of the covenant had been brought to Jerusalem and placed in a tent that David had pitched for it (see 1 Chronicles 16). David was always ready to praise God for all His providence. Are we as ready as he?

The psalm begins and ends with the same words. It is obvious that the psalmist is duly impressed with the excellence and majesty of God.

The Majesty of God's Name

The psalmist addresses God as Lord. The Hebrew word is *Jahweh,* the name that represents the "I am," the ever living God. The devout Israelite used this name when he recited the Shema, recorded in Deuteronomy 6:4, which says: "Hear, O Israel: the Lord our God, the Lord is one."

Jesus quoted the Shema when He told a teacher of the law which was the most important commandment (see Mark 12:28, 29). He began by identifying God. He is the only true God, the only God that you and I can serve, the only God that the psalmist had in mind. The apostle Paul emphasized this point when he said: "There are many 'gods' and many 'lords,' yet for us there is but one God, the Father, from whom all things came and for whom we live" (1 Corinthians 8:5, 6).

The psalmist makes the Lord very personal; he says: "O

Lord, our Lord" (verse 1). The emphasis on the pronoun is significant. The psalmist directs his hymn of praise to a God who is a God of all people—the psalmist, you, me, everyone. God is not a being so far away that we cannot know Him. He is not so distant that we cannot feel Him in our lives or see Him in His works. He has revealed Himself to us; He is ours, and we belong to Him.

"How majestic is your name." The word *majestic*, or *excellent* (KJV), tells us that God is high and exalted. Earthly potentates are "high" in the sense that it is difficult for the average citizen to reach them. Kings and queens are "high" in the sense that they are addressed as "Your majesty" and are usually treated with pomp and ceremony. God is high and exalted above any earthly potentate, above anything that we can think of; yet He can be reached. God is high in the sense that we should approach Him only with a sense of awe and respect.

God's name is the essence of His being. In biblical times names had special significance. For example, Abram meant "Father," and Abraham meant "Father of a multitude" (see Genesis 17:5). Jacob was a "supplanter," not only in name but also in character. Matthew tells us that *Jesus* means "Saviour" (see Matthew 1:21). Thus a biblical name is more than a means of identification; it is usually a reflection of character. To take God's name in vain, or to misuse His name, is not merely to mouth the name carelessly; it is to misrepresent His character. If we call ourselves "Christian," we must be sure that we are true followers of Christ.

The psalmist is asserting that God's whole being is majestic. When we consider His character and what He has done, we are struck with awe; we bow down with holy reverence.

"In all the earth." It does not matter where we are on the earth or during what period of time we live; God must be the Supreme Being to whom we give reverence and praise. The question that comes to us personally is this: Are we as conscious of God in our lives as we ought to be? Do we recognize His awesomeness? Or can it be that we are so taken up with our daily duties that we have no time for Him?

"You have set your glory above the heavens." God's splendor

is above the heavens, that is, beyond the reach of human conception. Jesus said: "No one has ever seen God" (John 1:18). It is only by the eye of faith and in the revelation of Jesus Christ that we can begin to "see" Him. Furthermore, God's glory is not limited to His outward splendor; it is revealed primarily in His character (see Exodus 33:19, 20).

Robert Grant expresses this thought in the words of a well-loved hymn:

> O worship the King, all glorious above,
> O gratefully sing His wonderful love;
> Our shield and defender, the Ancient of days,
> Pavilioned in splendor, and girded with praise.

Children in God's Kingdom

Generally speaking, we think of children as immature, helpless, in need of instruction. In a manner they are. We doubt whether they can play much part in God's kingdom. Yet Jesus said to His disciples: "I tell you the truth, unless you change and become like little children, you will never enter the kingdom of heaven" (Matthew 18:3).

What characteristics of children should we emulate? Children have the characteristic of humility. They are willing to learn and readily accept the teaching of their parents. We adults are more sophisticated. Experiences of life have taught us to be cautious, less trusting. In our Christian life, we do well to develop the simple characteristics of children and learn to be loving and trusting and willing to be taught. Only with these characteristics do we find ourselves entering the kingdom of heaven.

One time mothers brought their children to Jesus to have Him place His hands on them and bless them. The disciples thought that this interruption was an infringement on Jesus' time. Hence they urged the parents to take the children away. But Jesus said: "Let the little children come to me, and do not hinder them, for the kingdom of heaven belongs to such as these." Jesus then proceeded to bless them (see Matthew 19:13-15).

So often our concepts of the kingdom must be set straight. Perhaps we set too high a value on ourselves. Perhaps we have forgotten the simpler virtues and make life too complicated. We need to be like children who come to their parents with trust and so come to God with a willingness to learn and accept what has been revealed. Only then can we truly appreciate reality; only then can we be effective in the kingdom of truth and righteousness.

The psalmist surprises us by saying: *"From the lips of children and infants you have ordained praise"* (verse 2). The expression "ordained praise" seems to fit very well the reference to "lips," but the Hebrew word translated here as "praise" really means "strength" (see margin of NIV). Hence the JPS version translates it "founded strength." This makes the statement of the psalmist even more unexpected: strength from children?

Yet Jesus had this statement in mind when He said: "I praise you, Father, Lord of heaven and earth, because you have hidden these things from the wise and learned, and revealed them to little children. Yes, Father, for this was your good pleasure" (Matthew 11:25, 26).

Jesus found that the learned men of His day were not the ones who accepted Him. It was not they who could testify to God's goodness and power. Rather it was the poor and the uneducated who raised their voices in powerful testimony. Thus a man born blind who had been healed by Jesus could confound the Pharisees by his forceful testimony: "One thing I do know. I was blind but now I see!" (John 9:25). Again and again, it is not the sophistication of human reasoning that establishes God's truth; it is a simple statement of fact. Even a child can know what has happened to him or her.

The psalmist goes on to say, *"Because of your enemies."* Does God have enemies? Apparently He does! How does God handle His enemies? By the testimony of children, those who are apparently weak!

Paul was a learned man, a strong character. Yet he had a "thorn in the flesh"—apparently poor eyesight. He wanted to have this disability taken from him. But the Lord said to him:

"My grace is sufficient for you, for my power is made perfect in weakness (see 2 Corinthians 12:7-9). How often the values of earth are turned upside down by the values of heaven! God uses the weak to confound the mighty, the frail to accomplish His purposes.

Do you feel weak and helpless? Courage! God may still use you if you are willing to be used.

"To silence the foe and the avenger." God needs His enemies silenced, and He can use you and me to do it. In our sophisticated world we tend to set much store by wisdom, strength, and riches. God told Jeremiah, however, "Let not the wise man boast in his wisdom or the strong man boast of his strength or the rich man boast of his riches, but let him who boasts boast about this: that he understands and knows me, that I am the Lord, who exercises kindness, justice and righteousness on earth, for in these I delight" (Jeremiah 9:23, 24). Can it be that God can use us best when we are like children, believing in God, knowing Him and putting our trust in Him?

The Value of a Human Being

The psalmist makes a striking contrast between the magnitude of the universe and the comparative smallness of man. Such contrast brings out the true greatness of God.

Jesus made the contrast even greater. He said to the disciples: "Even the very hairs of your head are all numbered" (Matthew 10:30). It is not only a question of "Can He?" but "Does He?" "Yes, He can; Yes, He does," says Jesus.

The psalmist no doubt contemplated the heavens when he was a shepherd. At night he would see the moon and the stars. He would notice how the constellations revolved around the pole star. He would wonder how far away they might be. He had no means of knowing, of course, but he was impressed with their vastness.

The magnitude of the universe is only now being faintly realized. I say "faintly" because the figures used to represent space are staggering. We measure distance in light-years, that is, the distance by an object traveling at the speed of light,

186,282 miles a second, for a whole year. To get to the nearest star by rocket traveling about 19,000 miles per hour would take 144,000 years.

"*When I consider your heavens,*" says the psalmist (verse 3). It is doubtful that he was thinking in terms of a Big Bang theory of origins. He knew the story of creation recorded in Genesis, because the Pentateuch was available in his day. He believed that everything in the heavens was the work of a Creator God's "fingers." Sun, moon, and stars were placed there by Him. The vastness of the universe only made his concept of God greater.

Someone has said that the most important question in the Bible is, "What do you think about the Christ?" (Matthew 22:42). If this is so, then perhaps the second most important question is the question the psalmist asks: "*What is man?*" (verse 4). We need to know man's origin, his destiny, and how he can achieve his fullest potential.

Modern man usually thinks of humans as part of an evolutionary process. He assumes that man developed from very simple origins and gradually evolved into the very complex organism he is today. But the Bible gives us another picture of human beings. It is a picture of beings created in the image of God and placed in the Garden of Eden to have dominion over the earth, to be fruitful and multiply, and to live forever.

Unfortunately, man failed God. Adam and Eve sinned and became subject to death. The psalmist, when he asks, What is man? uses the Hebrew word *enosh*. In the Old Testament this word refers to mortal man, to man in his weakness. The psalmist is amazed that God would be "mindful" of such people. Why would God be interested in human beings, who have thrown away life and happiness?

The Hebrew word translated "mindful" is *zakar*, which means "to remember, to bring continually to mind." Thus God remembered Noah (see Genesis 8:1). God remembered Abraham (see Genesis 19:29). God continually remembers His covenant (see Exodus 6:5, 6). Thus God in His love continually keeps His children in mind and seeks to do them good. What a blessing it is that this is true! God keeps you and me ever in His mind to work for our best interests.

"The son of man." The word for *man* here is not *enosh* but adam. *Adam* is a generic name for humanity. In Genesis 1:27 we read: "God created man in his own image, in the image of God he created him; male and female he created them." We are the sons and daughters of Adam, and as such we are all equal in the sight of God. However, as descendants of Adam we have all inherited the sinful nature of our ancestor; we are all subject to death.

At the same time, it is important to note that Jesus called Himself by the title Son of man. With this title He affirmed His humanity. Yet He was also the Son of God. After the man born blind had been cured of his blindness, Jesus asked: "Do you believe in the Son of Man?" When the healed man wanted to know who that was, Jesus pointed to Himself. Immediately the man worshiped Him (see John 9:35-38). Jesus' acceptance of worship indicated that the title Son of man had a significance greater than that of a human relationship.

At Jesus' trial before the chief priests and the Sanhedrin, the high priest charged Him under oath to declare whether He was the Christ. He responded affirmatively and added: "In the future you will see the Son of Man sitting at the right hand of the Mighty One and coming on the clouds of heaven" (see Matthew 26:59-64). The high priest understood the implication of Son of man and reacted accordingly.

Jesus was saying that the Son of man and the Son of God were one and the same. His humanity did not negate His divinity. Furthermore, because He was without sin, death had no hold on Him. Thus the apostle Paul could make an important contrast: "Since death came through a man, the resurrection of the dead comes also through a man. For as in Adam all die, so in Christ will all be made alive" (1 Corinthians 15:21, 22). The Bible talks about a first Adam and a second Adam. Through the first Adam we inherited sinful natures; through the second Adam, Christ, we become new creatures. Paul's struggle with sinful nature caused him to cry out: "Who will rescue me from this body of death?" Then the answer came: "Thanks be to God—through Jesus Christ our Lord" (Romans 7:24, 25).

The writer to the Hebrews quotes Psalm 8 and gives it a Messianic interpretation. "We see Jesus," he says, "who was made a little lower than the angels, now crowned with glory and honor because he suffered death, so that by the grace of God he might taste death for everyone" (Hebrews 2:9).

The lesson we are to draw is that we are important in God's sight. People may despise us for lack of education or talent. We may begin to think that our lives are useless. But in God's sight no creature is too small or too insignificant to be the object of His love. The greatest danger we all face—the loss of self-esteem—is eliminated when we remember that we are of such infinite value to God that He gave His only Son, that whoever believes in Him will not perish but have eternal life (see John 3:16).

God's Assignment of Authority

It had been God's purpose that human beings should have dominion over "the fish of the sea and the birds of the air, over the livestock, over all the earth" (Genesis 1:26). Man lost that dominion when he sinned. The land was cursed, and the animals became wild and afraid. Man has become subject to the ravages of nature, plagued by animals that kill. He is at the mercy of locusts and other creatures that destroy the crops. Even today, with all the knowledge science has provided and the pesticides that are available, there is still much crop loss from weeds and insect pests.

It is not God's purpose that this lost dominion be permanent. Although Satan has tried to thwart God's purposes and has succeeded in bringing about death and destruction, Satan himself will be defeated. The promise was given in the very beginning: "He will crush your head, and you will strike his heel" (Genesis 3:15). Satan did his worst to Jesus on the cross, but Jesus rose from the dead on the third day and gained eternal victory for us. Paul could cry out: "Where, O death, is your victory? Where, O death, is your sting?" (1 Corinthians 15:55).

The psalmist tells us the extent of man's dominion. "*You*

put everything under his feet" (verse 6). This dominion is not to be interpreted as the right to exploit the environment. God does not exploit, but extends to all creatures His tender loving care. Man, being made in God's image, should recognize his responsibility to do the same. The trouble is that sin has warped man's outlook and made him think that he can use the earth selfishly.

Fortunately, some have a concern for the environment and seek by pressure and by legal means to prevent air and water pollution. But countering exploitation of natural resources is a constant struggle. Man selfishly seeks his own profit and rarely considers the effect of his activity on the environment. By this selfishness he fails to live up to the image of God and becomes a minion of Satan.

Did the psalmist grasp the full implication of his words? Perhaps not. He certainly did not know what you and I know who live in the twentieth century. But he certainly knew how to praise his God.

A Glad Refrain

"O Lord, our Lord, how majestic is your name in all the earth!" Beginning and ending a psalm with the same exclamation is not merely a poetic technique. It represented a psalmist's deep recognition of God's inestimable greatness. He looks at the starry heavens, and he sees God the Creator and marvels at His greatness. He looks at human beings and wonders at God's loving care in spite of their sinfulness, waywardness, and obstinacy. He recognizes that God wants the best for him and wants to give him authority and dominion. He knows that a time will come when God's purposes will be fulfilled.

You and I, by God's grace, must respond in the same way. Unworthy though we may be, God has not dealt with us according to our desserts. We recognize His lovingkindness and mercy, and we cry out with the psalmist: "O Lord, our Lord, how majestic is your name in all the earth!" Let all the redeemed say so. Amen!

Chapter 5
Proper Behavior: The Marks of a Man of God

Psalm 15

Life is full of questions. We want to know what to eat to stay healthy. We want to know how to raise our families. We want to know what to say in certain circumstances, such as hospital visits and funerals. Fortunate is the person who finds the right answers to his questions.

Because some matters are not worth worrying about, but others are very important, we need to be able to distinguish between the two categories. For instance, Jesus said that we should not worry about clothes or food. These are concerns of the worldly minded. We should, instead, seek first the kingdom of God and His righteousness, and everything else will be provided for us.

The psalmist begins his psalm with what at first glance looks like two questions. But in reality it is only one question asked in two different forms. This technique, called parallelism, is typical of Hebrew poetry.

A Meaningful Question

"Lord, who may dwell in your sanctuary? Who may live on your holy hill?" (verse 1).

We notice first that the question is addressed to God. The psalmist is wise enough to know that God is the source of all true knowledge. Such a recognition is the beginning of wisdom. Second, the question relates to the sanctuary and God's holy hill. In other words, it relates to a matter of vital impor-

49

tance—our standing before God. Third, the question recognizes that not everyone can abide in the sanctuary or live on God's holy hill. Fourth, the question asks about the qualifications of a person who would want to live with God throughout eternity.

When the psalmist asks "who?" he is really asking: "What are the characteristics of the man or woman who looks forward to living with God? How does that person live in the present?"

The words *sanctuary* and *holy hill* suggest worship. The psalmist wants to know what kind of person's worship is acceptable. We tend to think of worship as an activity we do morning and evening and one day a week, but the psalmist regards worship as involving the whole person and the whole life. Furthermore, the words *dwell* and *live* suggest a host and guest situation. For the psalmist God is a Person with whom one can have fellowship. The figure of speech of host and guest is fitting in the context of the Middle East, where in both ancient and modern times hospitality is a way of life.

While recognizing that people are all different, inner feelings and purposes frequently may be revealed by their behavior. How can people of God be distinguished from worldly people around them? The question points out the importance of behavior in determining destiny.

The psalm is not about salvation. We misunderstand the psalm if we think that it gives us a series of do's and don'ts whereby we can earn salvation. Salvation is a gift of God that comes through faith in Him.

If salvation is a gift, why do we have rules of conduct? These rules show how the person who is saved will naturally live. In response to salvation and God's goodness, he will behave according to the pattern outlined.

Appropriate Conduct

"He whose walk is blameless and who does what is righteous" (verse 2). Walking blamelessly and doing what is right refer to the same activity. Here again the poet uses parallelism to provide emphasis without tedious repetition.

Tamim, the Hebrew word for *blameless*, means "whole, complete, sincere." It is sometimes translated "perfect" and has the connotation of being free from all objection. Used in reference to both sacrifices and people, *tamim* describes Noah in Genesis 6:9.

To be *tamim* is not necessarily to be without sin. We are all sinners before God. Noah was perfect, and yet he sinned (see Genesis 9:21). The man who walks blamelessly is a forgiven sinner, but more than this, he is wholly sincere in all his relationships.

He is sincere in his relationship with God. He does not try to hide anything, because he knows that hiding from God is futile. He does not pretend to be what he is not. He simply comes to God just as he is and throws himself at the mercy of God. He is equally sincere in his relationship with his fellow man. Perfectly honest and open, he is a rare kind of person because most of us try to cover our faults. Associates appreciate this kind of honesty, which eliminates the need for competition.

A proper relationship with God will always lead to right action. That is why the psalmist adds: He *"does what is righteous."* The psalmist is not adding words merely for poetic effect. He is anxious to describe fully the kind of person who is acceptable to God.

The man and woman of God do not do the right thing because they want to gain favor with God. They do it because they find it in their hearts to do the right thing rather than the wrong. Their behavior arises out of a vertical relationship with God.

In order to do what is right, one has to have a clear concept of right and wrong. This means that one must know what God has said in His commandments, for God is the source of all moral judgment. Human beings have created many ethical codes, but God's people are guided by the standard of righteousness laid down by God.

This does not mean that God's people never make mistakes, never transgress God's law. But it does mean that they are quick to repent, quick to set matters right. Someone has rightly said: It is not the things we do or do not do that matter in life; it is the direction in which we are headed.

Control of the Tongue

"*Who speaks the truth from his heart.*" Speaking the truth is not always easy. How does one tell a patient that he or she has an incurable disease? That death may be imminent? Is it proper in such a case to be less than truthful? Perhaps the patient is already aware of a serious condition. In that case it does not help to beat around the bush. Of course, "hope springs eternal in the human breast." It is always right to be positive and encouraging. But a time comes when one must place oneself in the hands of God. One must face reality truthfully.

One kind of speaking the truth may be cruel. Some delight in speaking the truth, but they use truth cruelly. Is it right to hurt with the truth? For instance, a child may make a mistake. Perhaps it is a stupid mistake. Should the parent call the child "stupid"?

The truth should always be kind and helpful, building relationships of trust. That is why men and women of God speak the truth. But they speak the truth with sensitivity and understanding and show that they care and want to be helpful. Such an attitude will never hurt.

There is a time when the truth must be spoken. When a person is called to testify in court, he or she must speak the truth. The ninth commandment says: "You shall not give false testimony against your neighbor" (Exodus 20:16). Jesus added the concept that our language should be simple and straightforward. "Simply let your 'Yes' be 'Yes,' and your 'No,' 'No'; anything beyond this comes from the evil one" (Matthew 5:37).

But the man of God does more than speak the truth; he speaks the truth "from his heart." That is, he and the truth are one. What he says is what he means. Are we always as honest as this? Jesus taught His disciples that words alone do not count. Unless backed by deeds, they do not get one into the kingdom. "Not everyone who says to me, 'Lord, Lord,' will enter the kingdom of heaven, but only he who does the will of my Father who is in heaven" (Matthew 7:21).

James points out that we often fail in controlling our tongues. He refers to the tongue as a fire. "The tongue also is a fire, a world of evil among the parts of the body. It corrupts the whole person, sets the whole course of his life on fire, and is itself set on fire by hell" (James 3:6). The tongue is the means by which we praise God, but it can also be used to curse people (see James 3:9).

Honesty in Relationships

He *"has no slander on his tongue."* The emphasis here is on *slander.* Slander is a way of treating people. In Leviticus we read: "Do not go about spreading slander among your people" (19:16). The Hebrew has the connotation of searching for information and spreading it abroad—almost a form of spying. Joseph accused his brothers of doing this when they came to Egypt to buy food. While still unrecognized by his brothers, he said: "You are spies! You have come to see where our land is unprotected" (Genesis 42:9).

While it is sometimes legitimate to gather information about people, it is another to gather such information in order to gossip. It is only too true that bad news spreads faster than good news. People have itching ears for scandal, and such news is tainted with slander. Someone has truly said: "God and gossiping will not go together."

Ellen White has likened gossip to cannibalism. She has said: "We think with horror of the cannibal who feasts on the still warm and trembling flesh of his victim; but are the results of even this practice more terrible than are the agony and ruin caused by misrepresenting motive, blackening reputation, dissecting character?" (*Education*, p. 235).

The same writer is concerned about "unruly tongues among church members. There are false tongues that feed on mischief. There are sly, whispering tongues. There is tattling, impertinent meddling, adroit quizzing. Among the lovers of gossip some are actuated by curiosity, others by jealousy, many by hatred against those through whom God has spoken to reprove them" (*Testimonies*, vol. 5, p. 94). Thus we can see that the injunction against slandering is well taken. The man of God will keep well away from it.

"*Who does his neighbor no wrong and casts no slur on his fellow man.*" Obviously the psalmist is much concerned about relationships between people. God's people, who are anxious to worship God acceptably and live with Him throughout eternity, will make sure that they do not injure or harm anyone.

Today's English Version translates this passage as, "Does not spread rumors about his neighbors." The man of God is concerned about truth, not rumors. He wants facts, not hearsay. Furthermore, he is not interested in anything about his neighbor that is discreditable. He follows the advice of the wise man who says: "Hatred stirs up dissension, but love covers over all wrongs" (Proverbs 10:12).

The Christian recognizes that it is wise to follow the apostle Paul's advice: "Whatever is true, whatever is noble, whatever is right, whatever is pure, whatever is lovely, whatever is admirable—if anything is excellent or praiseworthy—think about such things" (Philippians 4:8).

"*Who despises a vile man*" (verse 4). That is, a person whom God rejects. Christians cannot condone vileness. We may feel sorry for a vile person, but we cannot approve of such a person's acts or speech. We may, like God, hope that he or she will change in attitudes and behavior, but if the person persists in disloyalty to God, then the Christian will withdraw from association with such a person. He does so as a mark of his own loyalty to God.

"*Honors those who fear the Lord.*" It is not surprising that the man of God honors those who, like himself, fear the Lord. He is attracted to them because they have similar interests, loyalties, dedication to truth. The psalmist is being specific when he uses the expression "fear the Lord." He is not referring merely to religious people. He means people who live in awe of God and have a strong relationship with Him.

To honor means "to show respect." The fifth commandment, "Honor your father and your mother," uses the same word to describe respect for parents. Do we show that kind of respect to fellow members of our church? Do we hold the church leaders in high regard? How do we regard our fellow Christians?

"Who keeps his oath even when it hurts." Here is a commitment of high worth. The man of God makes his word his bond; when he makes a promise he keeps it.

In our modern society we want a statement signed and notarized. We feel that verbal agreement is no longer an adequate guarantee. The reason for distrust is the frequency of people changing their minds and then denying their previous statements. Christians, however, are honest and straightforward. People who have dealings with them will soon see that they can be trusted to fulfill their obligations, even when keeping promises results in loss. Here is a type of behavior that is truly commendable.

Proper Use of Money

Few matters are more important to Christians than the way they use their wealth. Wealth can be addictive, as Jesus pointed out in His parable of the rich fool. "The ground of a certain rich man produced a good crop. He thought to himself, 'What shall I do? I have no place to store my crops.' Then he said, 'This is what I'll do. I will tear down my barns and build bigger ones, and there I will store all my grain and my goods. And I'll say to myself, "You have plenty of good things laid up for many years. Take life easy; eat, drink and be merry." ' But God said to him, 'You fool!' " (Luke 12:16-20).

There is nothing wrong in wealth per se. Wealth can be a sign of God's blessing. But wealth must not be handled selfishly, for it is given to be used to bless others.

The psalmist is concerned with two aspects of wealth:

(1) Lending money and taking advantage of the debtor; (2) accepting a bribe and thus perverting justice.

The first principle seems to be that if God has blessed you with more money than you need, then you have the privilege of helping out a person in need (see Exodus 22:25). You should not act like a moneylender and charge interest. On the other hand, if you are using your money in a business transaction and the borrower is making a profit from the deal, then it is perfectly proper to charge interest (see Deuteronomy 23:19, 20).

It is interesting to note that the root of the Hebrew word for *interest* means "to bite." If interest is something "bitten off," it is important to be careful whom and how we bite!

In our modern society the payment of interest is a recognized practice. Institutions that use our money, such as banks, pay interest for its use. They, in turn, lend the money to others and make a profit. So long as the terms of interest are well within reason, there can be no basis for objection. Scripture is not against making a profit; it warns against making an exorbitant profit and against making profit at the expense of the needy.

The second concern of the psalmist is the acceptance of bribes in order to pervert justice. The Christian will have nothing to do with this obvious evil.

The Bible mentions a number of cases of bribe-taking. The sons of Samuel the prophet accepted bribes (see 1 Samuel 8:3). In Psalm 26 we read of wicked men whose right hands are full of bribes (see verse 10). In the book of Job we read that "fire will consume the tents of those who love bribes" (Job 15:34). On the other hand, Isaiah promises blessings for those who refuse bribes: "He who walks righteously and speaks what is right, who rejects gain from extortion and keeps his hand from accepting bribes, who stops his ears against plots of murder and shuts his eyes against contemplating evil—this is the man who will dwell on the heights, whose refuge will be the mountain fortress. His bread will be supplied, and water will not fail him" (Isaiah 33:15, 16).

The psalmist closes his list of attributes of the man or woman of God with a strong assurance: *"He who does these things will never be shaken."* In the words of Today's English Version: he "will always be secure." Let us thank God for the security that He gives us, for the instruction that we receive from Him, and for the grace that enables us to live in accordance with His high standards of life in this world and that gives us the promise of life in the next.

Chapter 6
The Music of the Spheres: A Heart in Tune With God

Psalm 19

This psalm is attributed to David, the sweet singer of Israel. In reference to this psalm, C. S. Lewis has said: "I take this to be the greatest poem in the Psalter and one of the greatest lyrics in the world" (*Reflections on the Psalms* [New York: Harcourt, Brace and Company, 1958], p. 63).

The title of this chapter has been taken from a beloved hymn by Maltbie D. Babcock:

This is my Father's world,
And to my listening ears,
All nature sings, and round me rings
The music of the spheres.

Do we have listening ears? Do we hear the music of the spheres?

This is not the first time the psalmist has referred to the heavens. In Psalm 8 he compared the magnitude of the universe with the relative insignificance of man. In this psalm he deals with the message of the heavens.

The Heavens as a Manifestation of God's Glory

"The heavens declare the glory of God; the skies proclaim the work of his hands" (verse 1). The story is told of a Russian

astronaut who was asked whether he had seen God in his travels through space. Are we surprised at his negative reply? Of course he did not see God, for no man can see God and live (see Exodus 33:20). John in his Gospel declares: "No one has ever seen God, but God the only Son, who is at the Father's side, has made him known" (John 1:18).

The psalmist is not saying that we actually see God in the heavens. What we see is a manifestation of His glory. We see the magnificence and orderliness of the heavens, and we come to the conclusion that behind all this is a great Creator.

The apostle Paul makes a similar assertion in his letter to the Romans. He says that the Gentiles are without excuse if they have not come to a realization that there is a God. He says: "What may be known about God is plain to them, because God has made it plain to them. For since the creation of the world God's invisible qualities—his eternal power and divine nature—have been clearly seen, being understood from what has been made, so that men are without excuse" (Roman 1:19, 20).

Paul makes the following points: (1) The message of the heavens is plain, since God has made it plain. (2) The message has been clear ever since man has been on the earth. (3) What we see with our eyes must be "understood," that is, our minds must take us beyond the visible objects to the invisible Being who must be behind them. (4) Two characteristics of God are obvious: His ever-present power and His deity.

Granted that nature does not tell us everything about God, but it forms part of general revelation that can lead to a special revelation in the Word of God.

It is significant to note that in this first verse of the psalm, the psalmist uses three words that are found in the Genesis Creation story. Could it be that he had Genesis in mind?

"*Heavens.*" Genesis tells us: "In the beginning God created the heavens" (Genesis 1:1).

"*God.*" The word that the psalmist uses is *El.* The word that Genesis uses for God is *Elohim,* a plural form of *El.*

"*Skies.*" The Hebrew word used by the psalmist is *raki'a.* This is the same word used in Genesis for "firmament" (KJV) or "expanse" (NIV). Genesis says: "And God said: Let there be an expanse between the waters" (Genesis 1:6).

With this close similarity to Genesis 1 it seems evident that the psalmist had in mind a clear reference to God as the Creator.

"Day after day they pour forth speech; night after night they display knowledge" (verse 2). The heavens are like a book that can be read at any time—daytime or nighttime. Just as we find information in a book, so we can find knowledge as we scan the heavens and seek to understand what they have to say to us.

"There is no speech or language where their voice is not heard" (verse 3). With so many languages and dialects in the world we can understand one another only through translators. A foreign language is only so many sounds to our ears. In contrast, the heavens speak a universal language. It matters not what the native tongue; a man or woman can gaze at the heavens and receive a clear message of a Creator.

"Their voice goes out into all the earth, their words to the ends of the world" (verse 4). The margin of the NIV tells us that the translation "voice" is supported by the Septuagint, Jerome, and the Syriac. The Hebrew word is *line,* and this is the translation we have in the KJV. George A. F. Knight, in his commentary on the Psalms, makes the following interesting observation: "The Hebrew word seems to employ a pun which we can perhaps convey by saying that 'cord' can also be spelt as 'chord.' So we might even put it this way: Their tune has gone out . . ." (p. 94). If so, we get back to the music of the spheres!

In this context we may note the stanza in Joseph Addison's hymn which says:

> What though no real voice nor sound
> Amidst their radiant orbs be found?
> In reason's ear they all rejoice
> And utter forth a glorious voice,
> Forever singing as they shine,
> "The hand that made us is divine."

"In the heavens he has pitched a tent for the sun." In these words the psalmist makes it perfectly clear that the sun is not a god, contrary to the thinking of so many in the ancient world. In Egypt, the sun was the supreme God. In Mesopotamia, Shamash, the sun-god, was credited with giving to King Hammurabi the code of laws now known as the Code of Hammurabi. In the thinking of the psalmist, the sun is merely an object that God has placed in the sky to perform a particular task. Thus in Genesis we read: "And God said: 'Let there be lights in the expanse of the sky to separate the day from the night, and let them serve as signs to mark seasons and days and years' " (Genesis 1:14). More specifically we read: "God made two great lights—the greater light to govern the day and the lesser light to govern the night" (verse 16).

"Which is like a bridegroom coming forth from his pavilion, like a champion rejoicing to run his course" (verse 5). The imagery is of a sun that rises in the east ready for a new day's activity. There is no hesitancy, no delay. It seems to be eager to undertake its task.

"It rises at one end of the heavens and makes its circuit to the other; nothing is hid from its heat" (verse 6). In Palestine, where the psalmist lived, the sun could be very hot. Shade was a welcome spot in which to rest. Day after day the sun would rise and set, performing perfectly the task that God had assigned to it. It is interesting in this connection to note the words of Jesus: "God causes his sun to rise on the evil and the good" (Matthew 5:45). God provides the sun's light and warmth for everyone, thereby setting a pattern for Christians to be impartial in their relations with other people.

The Law as a Source of Wisdom and Joy

The psalmist may seem to be changing his topic in verse 7, but he is really on the same theme: the God who created the world and set it in motion is the same God who has laid down the rules for man's conduct. The God of general revelation is also the God of special revelation.

"The law of the Lord is perfect, reviving the soul" (verse 7). The Hebrew word the psalmist uses for *law* is *Torah*, an ex-

pression that includes more than the Decalogue; it refers to all the instruction given by God to the children of Israel and, through them, to all mankind. Hence the JPS version translates this word as "teaching."

The psalmist now uses the word *Yahweh* for God. Yahweh is the covenant-making and covenant-keeping God. He is the One who gave the Ten Commandments on Mount Sinai (see Exodus 20:1-17). He is the One who said through the prophet Jeremiah: "I will put my law in their minds and write it on their hearts. I will be their God, and they will be my people" (Jeremiah 31:33).

"Perfect," in Hebrew *Tamim.* We have come across this word before. It means "whole," "complete," "without blemish." God's law and teaching partake of His character. It revives or renews the soul. This idea may surprise us as Christians, since we remember the words of the apostle Paul: "Through the law we become conscious of sin" (Romans 3:20). Does consciousness of our sins revive us? Paul also admitted: "When the commandment came, sin sprang to life and I died" (Romans 7:9). Is this being renewed? Of course Paul also said: "The law is holy, and the commandment is holy, righteous and good" (Romans 7:12).

The value of the law is that it tells us what is right and what is wrong. In this regard we are not left in any quandary as to God's will. We know that we are sinners. We may cry out with Paul: "What a wretched man I am! Who will rescue me from this body of death?" Then the answer comes: "Thanks be to God—through Jesus Christ our Lord" (Romans 7:24, 25). We rejoice with Paul when he says: "There is no condemnation for those who are in Christ Jesus, because through Christ Jesus the law of the Spirit of life set me free from the law of sin and death" (Romans 8:1, 2).

The renewing comes when we are enabled to keep the law and are obedient to the commandments. Jesus said: "I have come that they may have life, and have it to the full" (John 10:10).

"The statutes of the Lord are trustworthy, making wise the simple." Statutes is a synonym for *laws.* They are trustworthy

and reliable. We can depend on what they say.

We may not like being called "simple," but all of us have been led astray into what we know to be wrong. God's teaching will bring us back into the ways of truth and righteousness. For this we may be truly thankful.

"The precepts of the Lord are right, giving joy to the heart" (verse 8). The psalmist uses the Hebrew word for *precepts* again and again (see Psalms 119:4; 103:18; 111:7). The reference seems to be to God's covenant with His people and His self-revelation in nature. God's provisions for people contain nothing crooked or misleading. They are right and proper, and we should accept them as reasonable. Furthermore, all God's dealings are gracious and kind, and that brings joy to our hearts.

"The commands of the Lord are radiant, giving light to the eyes." The psalmist continues his eulogy on God's requirements. We find that Psalm 119 contains a further listing of the benefits of God's word. Are we as conscious of the value of God's commands as he is?

Most of us do not like to be told what to do; we prefer to make our own decisions. We want to be free! But experience has shown that those of us who break God's laws end up being miserable. For instance, we cannot break the laws of health with impunity. We cannot use tobacco and alcoholic beverages and not reap the consequences of our behavior. Unfortunantly many people find the truth of this principle too late and must deal with the consequences. Fortunately, God is gracious and forgives us as we turn to walk in the path of obedience to God's commandments.

"Giving light to the eyes" means that God's precepts give us understanding. Then we know God's commands are like a lamp, and His teaching like a light to inform our journey through life (see Proverbs 6:23).

"The fear of the Lord is pure, enduring forever. The ordinances of the Lord are sure and altogether righteous" (verse 9). No life can be purer than a life lived in awe and reverence of God and in keeping the commandments. Such a life of purity and right doing will last throughout eternity.

"They are more precious than gold, than much pure gold" (verse 10). Do we recognize that the life of piety and service to God is worth more than the wealth of the world? Sometimes we need to have our priorities reversed. Thank God for the truths that we have in the Scripture.

"They are sweeter than honey, than honey from the comb." Perhaps we need to have our taste buds re-created! We can then enjoy the true and the lovely, rather than the flashy and the transient. We can rejoice in the Word of God rather than in the words of men. We can find life exhilarating and fun rather than dull and boring.

"By them is your servant warned, in keeping them there is great reward" (verse 11). Here we have the sum of the matter: God's teaching tells us the way that we should go. It also warns us of the consequences of disobedience. If we pay attention to what we are told, if we diligently walk in the path of truth, we shall receive a glorious reward. Would any of us really want to take a different road?

The Response of the Psalmist

"Who can discern his errors?" (verse 12). The psalmist knows the wonders of God's law. He knows the reward of taking the path of obedience. He knows that the world is God's world. Yet he sees that in God's world there are calamities, and he wonders why. He sees that so many do not seek to do God's will, and he wonders why. He looks inward and wonders whether he always does what is right.

The psalmist realizes that sin has caused changes in God's world. Could it be that sin has warped his own thinking as well as the thinking of many others? Perhaps things exist in his life of which he is not aware, things that would hinder his enjoying the great reward. Thus he asks for forgiveness.

"Forgive my hidden faults." The psalmist shows his awareness that a person can sin without knowing it. The law of sin offerings made provision for such sins, whether on behalf of an individual or of a group. Sin is sin, whether intentional or not, and needs to be atoned for with an appropriate sacrifice (see Leviticus 4; Numbers 15).

"Keep your servant also from willful sins; may they not rule over me" (verse 13). The Levitical code did not make provision for the atonement of willful sin, a sin that a person persevered in, regardless of the consequences. Because it was a kind of rebellion against God, the psalmist did not want to be guilty of that kind of sin.

At the same time he did not want to be caught guilty of committing the same sin again and again. He did not want to be held captive by sin, but wanted instead to be preserved from sin. His desire was to be free from every kind of sin, so that he would not miss the reward offered to God's faithful people.

"Then will I be blameless, innocent of great transgression." The Hebrew word for *blameless* is rooted in the word *tamim*, meaning "perfect," which we have met before. The psalmist wanted to be perfectly acceptable to God. He also wanted to be free from "the great transgression." The Hebrew for *transgression* is *pesha*, which means "an act in deliberate defiance of God's authority." The children of Israel committed a "great" sin when they worshiped the golden calf (see Exodus 32:21, 30, 31). The psalmist wants to be saved from committing the ultimate sin of rejecting God and falling into idolatry.

"May the words of my mouth and the meditation of my heart be pleasing in your sight, O Lord, my Rock and my Redeemer" (verse 14). The psalmist closes with words that are the prayer of every Christian, every believer.

Chapter 7
The Pain of Abandonment: The Triumph of Faith

Psalm 22

Psalm 22 is attributed to David, but scholars are at a loss to pinpoint any experience of David that would parallel the experience described in this psalm. Jesus quoted the words of the first verse when He was on the cross, and the psalm describes a number of scenes that took place at the crucifixion. Christians have come to regard the psalm as Messianic, best understood as a prophetic statement regarding Jesus and His experience on the cross.

The psalm contains two main emphases: the sufferings of Jesus and the triumph of His faith. There is no doubt about the sufferings of Jesus on the cross, but the psalm also points out that Jesus looked forward to a future glory when *all the ends of the earth will remember and turn to the Lord"* (verse 27).

The Pain of Feeling Abandoned

The first verse is a cry of agony: *"My God, my God, why have you forsaken me?"* The Gospels of Matthew and Mark both record that Jesus quoted this verse on the cross (see Matthew 27:46; Mark 15:34).

The Hebrew word translated *forsaken* is a strong verb suggesting abandonment. We know that Judas betrayed his master with a kiss, that the other disciples deserted Jesus and fled, that false witnesses testified at the illegal trial. The people who should have accepted Jesus as their Messiah cried out, "Crucify him!" and hurled insults at Him while He hung on the cross between two thieves. It is no wonder that He felt abandoned (see Mark 14:15).

"Why are you so far from saving me, so far from the words of my groaning?" We know that the chief priests and the teachers of the law and the elders mocked him with the words: "He saved others, but he can't save himself! He's the king of Israel! Let him come down now from the cross, and we will believe in him" (Matthew 27:41, 42). How cruel must have been those words to Jesus!

Yet we notice that Jesus retained His faith in the Father, even when expressing a feeling of abandonment. He addressed God as *my* God. He repeated the pronoun *my*. God was still His God even at a time of bitter pain and agony. Would that we maintain our hold on God even when our prayers seem to be unanswered. It is such faith that is victorious in the end.

Job's wife seemed to feel that her husband should curse God and die! Yet in the midst of circumstances of seeming abandonment, Job replied: "You are talking like a foolish woman. Shall we accept good from God, and not trouble?" (Job 2:10). Paul felt abandoned at his first trial (see 2 Timothy 4:16). But in writing to the church in Corinth, he said: "We who are alive are always being given over to death for Jesus' sake, so that his life may be revealed in our mortal body" (2 Corinthians 4:11).

Jesus' cry of abandonment on the cross indicates that the physical suffering, excruciating though it must have been, was not uppermost in His thoughts. His mind was fixed on God and on the task He had come to accomplish. Determined to glorify God, He maintained trust in God even through the bitterest moments.

The Antidote to Feelings of Despair

"Yet you are enthroned as the Holy One; you are the praise of Israel. In you our fathers put their trust; they trusted and you delivered them" (verses 3, 4). Jesus saw God as the Holy

One. He Himself bore the sins of the world, became a curse for us, and redeemed us from the curse of the law (see Galatians 3:13). "God made him who had no sin to be sin for us, so that in him we might become the righteousness of God" (2 Corinthians 5:21). Jesus recognized that God abhors sin. It is therefore understandable that He felt abandoned while bearing our sins on the cross. Yet even in His desolation Jesus retained confidence in God and the plan of salvation.

The Gospel records reveal that Jesus quoted the first verse of the twenty-second psalm, but it seems possible that He recited the entire psalm from time to time. Thus we have not merely an expression of abandonment, but also an expression of trust and understanding. Jesus looked back in history and saw how the Israelites had trusted in God and were delivered. He trusted that present deliverance was therefore certain, no matter how dark the appearances of evil may be around Him.

"They cried to you and were saved; in you they trusted and were not disappointed" (verse 5). Here we have the voice of confidence and trust. Jesus knew that His sacrifice would not be in vain. Yet He was well aware of His circumstances. While we look to heaven, we must never forget that we are here on earth. At the same time, we must not be so caught up in our circumstances that we fall into self-pity. There must be a balance in our thinking, facing the real issues in life but also recognizing the part that God must and does play in our experiences.

"But I am a worm and not a man" (verse 6). This self-depreciating statement sounds inappropriate for Jesus to say. But in Isaiah 41:14 we read: " 'Do not be afraid, O worm Jacob, O little Israel, for I myself will help you,' declares the Lord, your Redeemer, the Holy One of Israel." Jesus was associating Himself with man who, in his sinful state, is a sorry representation of what God wanted him to be. This lament is not self-depreciation; it is a recognition of the contrast between man's nothingness on the one hand, and God's graciousness on the other.

As the second Adam, Jesus had taken man's place. He had asked John the Baptist to baptize Him, not because He had sinned, but "to fulfill all righteousness" (Matthew 3:15). As man, therefore, and sin-bearer, He could be thought of figuratively as a lowly worm. Unfortunately, human beings usually tend to think of themselves more highly than they ought.

"*Scorned by men and despised by the people.*" This phrase reminds us of another prophecy of the Messiah's sufferings. In Isaiah 53 we read: "He was despised and rejected by men, a man of sorrows, and familiar with suffering. Like one from whom men hide their faces he was despised, and we esteemed him not. Surely he took up our infirmities and carried our sorrows. . . . He was pierced for our transgressions, he was crushed for our iniquities; the punishment that brought us peace was upon him, and by his wounds we are healed" (verses 3-5). This picture of the Messiah differed completely from the one popularly held in the days of Jesus.

"*He trusts in the Lord; let the Lord rescue him*" (verse 8). These arrogant words were used by the leaders in Israel about Jesus. What a remarkable fulfillment of prophecy! Little did they know how Jesus would be marvelously vindicated on the resurrection morning. Trust in God will never be a source of weakness, but a source of strength.

The Cruelty of Our Environment

"*Many bulls surround me; strong bulls of Bashan encircle me*" (verse 12). Can we visualize Jesus on the cross, looking around at the scene before Him, recognizing that most of the disciples had fled in fear? That those who stood there gazing at Him had only evil intentions in their hearts? They were like "bulls of Bashan," a particularly strong breed, terrifying and fierce.

We may have experienced occasions when we have felt surrounded by people with evil intentions, when we have felt as though life was no longer an option. We can always say: "If God be for us, who can be against us?" What may seem to be a defeat may often be the source of victory. Was not that the case at the cross?

"*I am poured out like water*" (verse 14). We shall never be able to fathom the depth of the agony that Jesus experienced on the cross. We can only begin to imagine the feeling of despair when His life stream began to ebb away. Death, the second death, meant total separation from His Father (see Revelation 20:6).

Ellen White has described the scene on the cross in the following words:

> The spotless Son of God hung upon the cross, His flesh lacerated with stripes; those hands so often reached out in blessing, nailed to the wooden bars; those feet so tireless on ministries of love, spiked to the tree; that royal head pierced by the crown of thorns; those quivering lips shaped to the cry of woe. And all that He endured—the blood drops that flowed from His head, His hands, His feet, the agony that racked His frame, and the unutterable anguish that filled His soul at the hiding of His Father's face— speaks to each child of humanity, declaring, It is for thee that the Son of God consents to bear this burden of guilt; for thee He spoils the domain of death, and opens the gates of Paradise (*The Desire of Ages*, p. 755).

Surely our hearts respond in the words of Isaac Watts: "Love so amazing, so divine, / Demands my soul, my life, my all."

The Jews never practiced crucifixion, an incredibly cruel form of inflicting death, although as a mark of shame they might hang a dead body on a tree (see Deuteronomy 21:22). Used by the Medes, Persians, and Assyrians, crucifixion then reached the Phoenicians, who taught it to the Romans.

We shudder to think of the nails being driven into the flesh. How would the psalmist think of such torture when he says, *"They have pierced my hands and my feet"* (verse 16), unless he had clear prophetic insight?

Jesus showed the wounds in His hands as evidence of His resurrection. Thomas, doubting Thomas we call him, said: "Unless I see the nail marks in his hands and put my finger where the nails were, and put my hand into his side, I will not believe it" (John 20:25). A week later Jesus appeared before the disciples and told Thomas to put his finger in the nail print and his hand into His side. Thomas responded: "My Lord and my God!" The scars from crucifixion were a means of bringing belief to a human heart. Jesus added: "Because you have seen me, you have believed; blessed are those who have not seen and yet have believed" (verses 28, 29).

Victims of a crucifixion usually would hang on the cross for days before dying. The fact that Jesus died on Friday afternoon after just a few hours on the cross surprised the authorities. The Jews did not want the bodies left on the three crosses during the Sabbath and asked Pilate to have the thieves' legs broken to prevent their escape. Because Jesus had already died, the soldiers did not break His legs but simply confirmed His death with a spear thrust (see John 19:31-37). A requirement of the Passover lamb, which pointed forward to the Messiah, was that none of its bones should be broken (see Exodus 12:46). The soldiers' not breaking Jesus' legs fulfilled one prophecy about the Lamb who would take away the sins of the world (see John 1:29).

"They divide my garments among them and cast lots for my clothing" (verse 18). Jesus could see the soldiers responsible for the crucifixion dividing His clothes among themselves. Unconcerned about the person dying on the cross, they thought only about how they might profit from His clothing. Jesus had few material possessions to pass on to others; what He had to give was His life, a ransom for many.

The remarkable correlation between details foretold in the psalm and their fulfillment on crucifixion Friday is an outstanding example of biblical prophecy. Only by divine revelation could David have written what he did, thus providing additional evidence for the inspiration of the Word of God.

The Prayer of Faith

"But you, O Lord, be not far off; O my Strength, come quickly to help me" (verse 19). In spite of appearances, in spite of pain, Jesus never let go of His faith in God. The writer to

the Hebrews says: "During the days of Jesus' life on earth, he offered up prayers and petitions with loud cries and tears to the one who could save him from death, and he was heard because of his reverent submission." The writer goes on: "Although he was a son, he learned obedience from what he suffered and, once made perfect, he became the source of eternal salvation for all who obey him" (Hebrews 5:7-9).

In this comment we see clearly the humanity of Jesus. He dreaded death because it meant separation from His Father. His prayers were mixed with tears. Yet He never let go His faith in God, and God heard Him. Answers to prayers are not always immediate. For Jesus, the answer to His prayer came on the day of resurrection.

"Deliver my life from the sword, my precious life from the power of the dogs" (verse 20). It is natural for us to want to be saved from all calamities. We offer our prayers in faith, knowing that God will allow only what is best for us. Therefore, we end our prayers with a "Thy will be done." Prayer is not a means of escaping difficulties; it is communion with God in which we express our desires, but we let God have His way with us.

"Rescue me from the mouth of the lions" (verse 21). God did this for Daniel—and He can rescue us too. In asking, we show our faith that God is all powerful. At the same time, we submit our wills to God's will because we want God's truth to triumph.

The Road of Complete Trust

"I will declare your name to my brothers" (verse 22). With this verse the mood of the psalm changes. The topic is the same—Jesus and His work for us. But the plea for deliverance from suffering shifts to an expression of praise.

The writer to the Hebrews quotes verse 22 in the context of Jesus' proclaiming God's name or character among His "brothers." "Both the one who makes men holy and those who are made holy are of the same family" (Hebrews 2:11). What a privilege it is to belong to the family of Jesus! In spite of all our faults and failings, Jesus is not "ashamed" to call us members of His family. Amazing grace!

Not everyone of the human race is part of Jesus' family; only those who are sanctified, made "holy," are related to Him. Jesus prayed that we may be sanctified by the truth (see John 17:17). God's Word is truth, and as we study the Word of God, we are placing ourselves in the line of sanctification.

"In the congregation I will praise you." The word *congregation* applies to any gathering of people, but the writer to the Hebrews uses in his quotation a Greek word that means "church," (see Hebrews 2:12). The Christian appreciates the beautiful concept that Jesus is with us in the church, identifying with us and praising God. Are we as conscious of the presence of Jesus as we ought to be?

"He has not despised or disdained the suffering of the afflicted one" (verse 24). Here we have strong reason to praise God; He is ever mindful of those of us who are passing through difficulties and hardships. He hears our cries for help. James advises: "Brothers, as an example of patience in the face of suffering, take the prophets who spoke in the name of the Lord" (James 5:10). In the conflict with evil, suffering seems to be inevitable.

"The poor will eat and be satisfied" (verse 26). Here is a promise in which you and I can have a part. As we see the poor and needy, we can extend to them the helping hand. Thus all God's children will receive the blessings of having had their needs fulfilled, on the one hand, and being the instruments of God's favor, on the other. Are we living up to our responsibilities?

"For dominion belongs to the Lord and he rules over the nations" (verse 28). This assurance of God's control should give us confidence in a world containing so much wickedness. Sometimes we ask where God is when a natural disaster or a famine affects so many innocent people. We need to remember that death is not the greatest tragedy; the greatest continuing tragedy is neglecting to be right with God. We need to be at peace with God, recognizing that evil does exist, but the day will come when all evil and evildoers will be destroyed.

"Posterity will serve him" (verse 30). It is encouraging to

know that the time will come when people will serve the Lord, even though few serve Him now. Habakkuk promises: "The earth will be filled with the knowledge of the glory of the Lord, as the waters cover the sea" (Habakkuk 2:14). Such promises enable us to sing with hope:

> Jesus shall reign where'er the sun
> Does its successive journeys run;
> His kingdom stretch from shore to shore,
> Till moons shall wax and wane no more.

John the Revelator heard a seventh angel sounding his trumpet and loud voices in heaven saying: "The kingdom of the world has become the kingdom of our Lord and of his Christ, and he will reign for ever and ever" (Revelation 11:15).

"Future generations will be told about the Lord." Jesus promised that "this gospel of the kingdom will be preached in the whole world as a testimony to all nations, and then the end will come" (Matthew 24:14). John in vision saw "another angel flying in midair, and he had the eternal gospel to proclaim to those who live on the earth—to every nation, tribe, language and people" (Revelation 14:6). This message is being proclaimed now by God's people. God grant that we may be faithful in delivering this message until the whole world is warned and Jesus may come.

"For he has done it" (verse 31). This triumphant cry tells us that Jesus on the cross has provided eternal salvation for us. It rings as true as the words of Jesus on the cross: "It is finished" (John 19:30). It is for you and me to accept the plan of salvation so that we can join in the celebration of God's final victory.

God forbid that you or I should be so foolish as to ignore what God in Christ has done for us and lose the salvation that is so freely and graciously offered.

Chapter 8
The Lord Is My Shepherd

Psalm 23

The twenty-third psalm is attributed to David. Surely his masterpiece, it has been called the "pearl of the psalter." Why is there so much interest in it? What is its appeal?

The imagery of a shepherd and his sheep is best understood by one who is acquainted with the work of a shepherd and the nature of sheep. In our Western urbanized society, we have no contact with sheep and may never have seen a shepherd. Nevertheless, the psalm remains popular with Christian and Jew alike. Anyone familiar with the Scripture will have come across the metaphor of sheep and shepherds again and again.

The Shepherd and His Care

David knew what it was like to be a shepherd. As a lad he had looked after his father's sheep. He led them out of the fold in the morning, and he brought them back in the evening. He stayed with them in the fields all night during the spring and the fall, when the weather was pleasant. He knew each of them by name, and they recognized his voice. Because he knew how dependent they were on him, he took a special interest in the weak ones and the lambs, even carrying a lamb or a wounded sheep on his shoulders.

Probably David wrote this psalm toward the end of his life. Then he not only knew what it was like to look after sheep, but he could see how God had provided for him throughout his life. As a lad he had been chosen to be king. As a young man he had had to flee from Saul's jealous rages. He had fought with Goliath in the name of the Lord Almighty and gained a signal victory. He had become king with all the responsibilities that the office entailed. Even though he had failed many times, every time he had repented of his mistakes. As he thought of God's leading in his life, David could think of no better image than that of a shepherd.

"The Lord is my shepherd" (verse 1). David addresses God as Lord, Jahweh. Jahweh was the one who had called Abram out of Ur of the Chaldees (see Genesis 12:1). It was Jahweh who said to Abram: "Do not be afraid, Abram. I am your shield, your very great reward" (Genesis 15:1). It was Jahweh who changed Abram's name to Abraham, a name that meant "father of many nations" (Genesis 17:5). It was Jahweh who had appeared to Moses in the burning bush (see Exodus 3:2). It was Jahweh who had brought the children of Israel out of Egypt with signs and great wonders. It was Jahweh who had proclaimed the law on Mount Sinai and led the children of Israel into the Promised Land. This same Jahweh had chosen David to be king of Israel. To David, Jahweh was not only the One God (see Deuteronomy 6:4). He was the God of Israel, the God of history. There was no other than He.

No doubt David had meditated about this God. As he looked up into the heavens, he could not but be impressed with the Creator God. As he thought of the events of his life, he could see that God was with him. How could he best describe this God? By a stroke of genius, he called Him a shepherd. He could see that God had been to him what he himself had been to the sheep on the hills of Bethlehem. He was a caring God.

David personalizes his relationship with God; he says that the Lord is *his* God. Identifying God with the personal pronouns *my*, *I*, and *me* makes the psalm fit everyone. The Lord is your shepherd and mine. Do we recognize the importance of that personal touch? Because God is so accessible, you and I can rejoice in an individual relationship with Him.

"I shall lack nothing." David no doubt recognized that there were good shepherds and bad. He had been a good shepherd because the sheep belonged to his family and he cared about

them. Some shepherds were hirelings who cared only for their pay and refused unless forced to endure discomfort for the sake of the sheep.

Jesus referred to Himself as the "good shepherd" (see John 10:14). The good shepherd is characterized by his willingness to die for the sheep (see verse 11). The sheep are not afraid of anything because they know that all their needs will be supplied.

How are people like sheep? Jesus looked upon the people in His day, with their diseases and helplessness, and He said they were "like sheep without a shepherd" (Matthew 9:36). Is our situation very different today? You and I are in constant need of guidance and protection. We need our daily bread. We need health and strength to do our work. We need healing when we are sick. We need comfort when we are alone. We need God in every turn of our lives. Thank God He is a good shepherd, that He takes a personal interest in every one of us, that, with Him, we lack nothing.

This does not mean that we have everything we want. Unfortunately, many things that we want are not good for us. That is why Paul says in his letter to Timothy: "Godliness with contentment is great gain" (1 Timothy 6:6). He goes on to say: "People who want to get rich fall into temptation and a trap and into many foolish and harmful desires that plunge men into ruin and destruction" (verse 9). We can be thankful that God helps us escape these dangers, and live peaceful and contented lives.

A Life of Comparative Ease

"He makes me lie down in green pastures" (verse 2). One of the duties of the shepherd is to lead his sheep to suitable grazing land. He may have to travel for miles to find it, but he knows that it is absolutely essential for his sheep to have good food.

God our Shepherd has provided us with life. He gives us a mind to help us differentiate between good and evil. He accepts us when we give our hearts to Him, and He helps us as we develop our talents for useful service. Then He opens doors of opportunity so that we can serve Him. Have you noticed how important God's provision is in every phase of our lives?

Some people never think of God, never seem to realize how important He can be in their lives. God is gracious to them as He is to us all. But when we remember that God is our Shepherd, we can be confident of His constant care and protection, realizing that He will lead us into green pastures.

"He leads me beside quiet waters." Did you know that sheep do not like to drink from running water? They like quiet water, pools where they are safe as they drink. So the shepherd must create quiet pools if the nearby stream has none.

Water is a basic necessity of life. We can last for many days without food, but only a few days without water. Perhaps that is why Jesus used the metaphor of water when He spoke to the woman of Samaria. He said, referring first to the water in the well and then to the Water of Life: "Everyone who drinks this water will be thirsty again, but whoever drinks the water I give him will never thirst. Indeed, the water I give him will become in him a spring of water welling up to eternal life" (John 4:13, 14).

Have you tasted cool water on a hot day? How refreshing it is! Jesus said: "If anyone gives a cup of cold water to one of these little ones because he is my disciple, I tell you the truth, he will certainly not lose his reward" (Matthew 10:42). But more important, you and I have an invitation: "The Spirit and the bride say, 'Come!' Whoever is thirsty, let him come; and whoever wishes, let him take the free gift of the water of life" (Revelation 22:17). The Good Shepherd invites us to quench our thirst with the Water of Life.

"He restores my soul" (verse 3). The psalmist seems to have set aside his imagery of sheep for a moment, but God the Good Shepherd is still there to provide our needs. He sees each one of us as a person, and He restores our energies, revives our spirits, and renews us for the struggles that may lie ahead.

How often we become discouraged with our situation, depressed with our circumstances—we wonder whether we can make it through life! Then God brings us a thought, a message, an insight, and we are pulled out of our lethargy and given a new impulse to move forward to courage and faith.

"He guides me in paths of righteousness for his name's sake." You and I need to be guided at all times. How grateful we can be for parents and teachers who have laid the foundation for the faith that we hold today. How often we have opened our Bibles and found the instruction that we needed! We have opened our hearts to God in prayer, and He has spoken to us words of encouragement and enlightenment. We must indeed be grateful to our Shepherd God, who guides into right paths, into paths of usefulness.

"For his name's sake" means "Because of who He is." Our God's character and promises are always consistent. He desires the very best for us and will never let us down. This does not mean that we never have to pass through difficult experiences. Because of sin, we will experience times of sorrow, times of helplessness, times of loss of loved ones. But in it all we may see God caring for us and not letting us fall into circumstances too difficult for us to bear.

The Comfort of Rod and Staff

"Even though I walk through the valley of the shadow of death" (verse 4). The story is told of a mother who came with her baby boy to a wise man and asked him to tell her what the future of that boy might be. The wise man showed his wisdom when he replied: "I can be sure of only one thing; your boy will die."

One of the consequences of sin, death has reigned from Adam's time down to our own. No death has been easy for loved ones to bear. The psalmist tells us that death is like a dark valley, a shadow that lies over us. His imagery was based on the many valleys in Palestine that were frequently the haunt of robbers who fell on unsuspecting travelers. David knew what it was like to walk through such a dark valley.

We may expect to pass through dark valleys in our lives. When it comes to death, however, we need not fear, for Jesus likened death to sleep. The disciples misunderstood our Lord, but Jesus made His reference clear (see John 11:11-14). Thus death need not hold any terror for us. John the Revelator emphasizes this point when he says: "I heard a voice from heaven say, 'Write: Blessed are the dead who die in the Lord from now on'" (Revelation 14:13).

"*I will fear no evil, for you are with me.*" Consciousness of the presence of God makes all the difference in our lives. When we know that God is with us, we have no reason to fear. Jesus left His disciples this promise: "Surely I will be with you always, to the very end of the age" (Matthew 28:20).

"*Your rod and your staff, they comfort me.*" The shepherd's rod was a kind of club that he could use to fight off marauding animals. To the sheep, the rod symbolized protection and reassurance that the shepherd had the means of warding off intruders. When David wanted to persuade Saul that he could tackle Goliath in combat, he said: "Your servant has been keeping his father's sheep. When a lion or a bear came and carried off a sheep from the flock, I went after it, struck it and rescued the sheep from its mouth. When it turned on me, I seized it by its hair, struck it and killed it" (1 Samuel 17:34, 35). David certainly had experience defending the sheep with his rod.

The shepherd used his staff for an entirely different purpose. He used it to help himself over difficult ground, and more important, to urge on lagging sheep. He would latch the curved end around the neck of a straying sheep and pull it back onto the right path. To this day, the bishops of some Christian communions carry a crook as a symbol of their office.

Both rod and staff brought comfort to the sheep because they were used for the sheep's benefit. We may be similarly secure, knowing that God has adequate means of warding off danger and bringing us back into the fold. Discipline of God's staff may be unpleasant, but it comforts us with the assurance of His concern. The writer to the Hebrews rightly says: "No discipline seems pleasant at the time, but painful. Later on, however, it produces a harvest of righteousness and peace for those who have been trained by it" (Hebrews 12:11).

The Life of Superabundance
With verse 5 the psalmist seems to set aside the metaphor

of shepherd and sheep. He now speaks of a host and his guest. The host is God; the guest is the psalmist. The change in imagery does not make any significant change in the message conveyed. God is still the Provider, while man is the recipient.

In the Middle East, the host takes it upon himself to feed the guests. This explains Abraham's making the necessary arrangements to entertain his three visitors (see Genesis 18:6-8). Very often the host will not eat except to show that the food is good. He urges everyone to partake of the meal and makes sure that there is plenty of food.

"You prepare a table before me in the presence of my enemies" (verse 5). Among the Bedouin tribes, a guest is always safe at his host's table. The host will always ensure his protection. David is not unmindful that he is living in a world abounding with enemies who would like to harm him. But so long as he is with God and God is with him, he has no reason to fear.

"You anoint my head with oil; my cup overflows." Once again we see a picture of Eastern hospitality in the practice of offering perfume or scented oils to the guest. Jesus attended a dinner given in His honor in Bethany. As He was reclining at the table, Mary brought some expensive perfume and poured it on Jesus' feet. When Simon criticized Jesus for allowing Mary to touch Him, Jesus gently rebuked Simon. He pointed out that Simon had neglected the courtesy of putting oil on His head, even though He was the guest of honor (see Luke 7:36-47; John 12:1-8).

The overflowing cup, like the spread table, is a symbol of God's generosity. He wants us to have enough and to spare. In the Middle East the cup is filled to the brim on the occasion of a feast. It may overflow, but the host is not niggardly; he has provided plenty more to drink. By the overflowing cup, he says to his guest: "Drink your fill. I want you to enjoy everything provided; there is plenty more if you need it."

One other aspect of Middle East hospitality enriches the host-and-guest imagery. To eat at a person's table is to establish a bond of trust and confidence that lasts throughout life. What a beautiful picture this is of God's generosity and care.

The Response of Faith

"Surely goodness and love will follow me all the days of my life" (verse 6). The Hebrew word for *follow* here has the connotation of "pursuing." God pursues us with goodness and love. He will not let us go. Even though at times we may reject Him, God remains ready to forgive and forget. Even though we may not deserve His many mercies, God is still merciful. He will pursue us to the end of our lives, ever wooing us to Himself. Such love is immeasurable and beyond compare! Do we respond with the psalmist and reach out and accept God's hand?

"I will dwell in the house of the Lord." The psalmist's ambition is not to be self-fulfilled. He does not desire to be great and do great things. Instead, he wants to remain ever in God's presence, to do those things that are pleasing to Him.

Can this be our experience today? The answer depends on us and our decisions. Jesus said: "If anyone chooses to do God's will, he will find out whether my teaching comes from God or whether I speak on my own" (John 7:17). In other words, God does not leave us in darkness as to what we ought to do. He makes the way plain, and it is up to us to follow His directions.

"Forever." This word stands by itself for emphasis, pointing to eternity. Our lives on this world may be short, but God's purpose is that we enjoy Him forever. Do you react to this promise with gratitude and praise?

Chapter 9
Waiting in Hope: The Secret of Success

Psalm 27

The word *waiting* is used in the heading of this chapter because the psalmist exhorts us to *"wait for the Lord"* (verse 14). The Jerusalem Bible translates the Hebrew, "Put your hope in." We wait in hope, eagerly expecting the coming of our Lord. When this expectation motivates our lives, we have nothing to fear and everything good to expect.

David begins this psalm by giving the reasons why he has no need to fear. He does so by asking rhetorical questions.

Antidote to Fear

"The Lord is my light and my salvation—whom shall I fear?" (verse 1). The psalmist personalizes his relationship with God. God is *his* light and *his* salvation. God is someone he knows, someone with whom he can communicate, someone who provides him with what he needs. The psalmist addresses God as *"Lord"* Jahweh, the ever-present, covenant-keeping God. Listen to the strong assertion of faith; the psalmist does not need to fear because the Lord is his light and his salvation. Let us look at these terms individually:

Light. Perhaps we fear nothing more than darkness. We feel helpless when we can see nothing around us. But God can throw light on every aspect of our lives. We have nothing to fear when He illumines our way.

Contrary to the thinking of the surrounding nations, the psalmist does not consider the sun the primary source of light.

He knows that it was God who created the sun and placed it in position to serve a definite function: to rule the day and to mark seasons and years (see Genesis 1:14-18).

The psalmist knew that it was the Lord who went ahead of the Israelites as they traveled to the Promised Land. God was in a "pillar of cloud to guide them on their way and by night in a pillar of fire to give them light" (Exodus 13:21). In Psalm 36 the psalmist acknowledges God as the source of all true light: "In your light we see light" (verse 9).

In later years the prophet Isaiah would say: "Come, O house of Jacob, let us walk in the light of the Lord." In another passage he said: "The Lord will be your everlasting light" (Isaiah 2:5; 60:20).

Some seven hundred years later Jesus would announce: "I am the light of the world. Whoever follows me will never walk in darkness, but will have the light of life" (John 8:12). John tells us in his first letter: "This is the message we have heard from him and declare to you: God is light." He goes on to say: "If we walk in the light, as he is in the light, we have fellowship with one another, and the blood of Jesus, his Son, purifies us from all sin" (1 John 1:5, 7).

As Christians, then, we have the privilege of walking in light. We understand where we came from, why we are here, and where we are headed. We know the truth, and the truth is liberating.

Salvation. This word implies distress. We are in the land of the enemy, but God has made provision for our deliverance. The psalmist no doubt knew the words of Moses: "Blessed are you, O Israel! Who is like you, a people saved by the Lord?" (Deuteronomy 33:29).

Another psalmist expresses similar trust: "I do not trust in my bow, my sword does not bring me victory; but you give us victory over our enemies, you put our adversaries to shame" (Psalm 44:6, 7). David knew that it was not his prowess or skill that saved him from his enemies; it was the Lord Himself.

Frequently evil forces are more formidable than human enemies. But God can deliver us from them as well. Paul points out that "our struggle is not against flesh and blood, but against the rulers, against the authorities, against the powers of this dark world and against spiritual forces of evil in the heavenly realms" (Ephesians 6:12). God will save us from these elements when we place our trust in Him. Thus we may say with the psalmist, the Lord is our light and salvation. We have nothing to cause us to be afraid.

"The Lord is the stronghold of my life—of whom shall I be afraid?" The psalmist has another reason for not being afraid; God is for him a "stronghold." The psalmist is confident, for God is his protection. Luther illustrated this confidence in the words of his famous hymn:

> A mighty fortress is our God,
> A bulwark never failing;
> Our helper He, amid the flood
> Of mortal ills prevailing.

Two New Testament texts may be cited as an antidote to fear. The first records the words of Jesus: "Do not be afraid, little flock, for your Father has been pleased to give you the kingdom" (Luke 12:32). The other records the words of John: "There is no fear in love. But perfect love drives out fear" (1 John 4:18). When we love God and keep His commandments, we have no reason to fear. On the contrary, we can rejoice in a God of love who is our stronghold.

The psalmist draws a remarkable picture in the second verse of the psalm: *"When evil men advance against me to devour my flesh, when my enemies and my foes attack me, they will stumble and fall."* The Lord does not simply offer protection; He annihilates the enemy! Could we ask for anything more to assure us of deliverance?

You and I may not see the foes that surround us. We may not see the protecting angels that surround us. We may be like Elisha's servant, who needed his eyes opened to see the chariots of fire that protected the prophet from his earthly foes (see 2 Kings 6:15-17). But we may be sure that God is our ring of protection—our stronghold, our fortress, our shelter.

In the third verse the psalmist says: *"Though an army be-*

siege me, my heart will not fear; though war break out against me, even then will I be confident." I like the word *confident*. It means that the psalmist has full trust in God's promises. He is not worried; he is not afraid. God is there, willing and able to give him all the protection he needs.

A Worthy Objective

"One thing I ask of the Lord, this is what I seek: that I may dwell in the house of the Lord all the days of my life" (verse 4). The psalmist, as king of Israel, had many matters calling for his time and attention. Yet he had one aim and ambition: to be with God in prayer and meditation. He was lonely for God.

Do we take time in our busy schedules to be alone with God? Do we recognize the importance of the quiet hour when we can commune with God? Or do the responsibilities of life drag us from one activity to another? If so, we shall soon feel a hunger that must be satisfied. We shall long as the psalmist did to be able to go aside and rest awhile. That is why we have the Sabbath day—to set aside the business of the week and to commune with God.

We remember the story of Jesus being entertained in Mary and Martha's home. Mary had decided to sit at the feet of Jesus and learn from Him. When Martha, busy with meal preparations, solicited Jesus' help in getting Mary to assist her, Jesus pointed out her need to balance priorities. "Martha, Martha . . . you are worried and upset about many things, but only one thing is needed. Mary has chosen what is better, and it will not be taken away from her" (Luke 10:41, 42). One thing is needed! We must find time for meditation and prayer. We must learn of Jesus.

Paul expressed clear goals and priorities in his letter to the Philippians: "One thing I do: forgetting what is behind and straining toward what is ahead, I press on toward the goal to win the prize for which God has called me heavenward in Christ Jesus" (Philippians 3:13, 14).

"To gaze upon the beauty of the Lord and to seek him in his temple." Has an object ever so fascinated you that you wanted to keep it forever before your eyes? "A thing of beauty is a joy

forever," says the poet. The beauty of the Lord is not external, like the beauty of a diamond. The psalmist is not attracted to the externals, but rather to the character of God.

What is the beauty that the psalmist expects and longs to see in the temple? It is not architecture or attractive furnishings. The temple had not been built in the days of the psalmist. The psalmist wanted to dwell upon God's gracious provision for man's salvation.

While it is true that we face many experiences that we cannot understand, the time comes when we must leave our affairs in God's hands, trusting in His goodness and love. The apostle Paul, learned scholar and theologian, exclaimed: "Oh, the depth of the riches of the wisdom and knowledge of God! How unsearchable his judgments, and his paths beyond tracing out!" (Romans 11:33).

The truths expressed in God's revelation will challenge the keenest mind, the most learned scholar. David delighted in trying to understand God's ways, yet he never felt that he had arrived, that he could fully explain the circumstances of life. The evidence he had was sufficient to maintain full confidence in God. Blessed are we when we recognize our limitations and are willing to trust God and place our affairs in His hands.

A Safe Refuge

"For in the day of trouble he will keep me safe" (verse 5). Who does not have days of trouble? Who does not face problems? As long as we are in the world, and as long as sin exists, we must expect trouble. The question is: How do we relate to our problems? Do they upset us? Do they make us think that God is far away and cannot help us? Do we blame God for our situations? The privilege of being a Christian is not that we are free from troubles but that God is at our side to help as we encounter and overcome them.

"He will . . . set me high upon a rock." God does more than put His arms around us to protect us; He sets our feet on a rock. More than that! *"High upon a rock."* To be on a rock is to be in a position of strength and stability. To be high upon the rock must suggest maximum stability. We may gather from

this passage that God is not satisfied with half measures; He always provides the best.

Are we as mindful of God's blessings as we ought to be? Do we recognize the reasons we have to rejoice in the God of our salvation? Perhaps we need to pray that God will open our eyes to all His providences, and then we will never fail to praise Him. God always treats us better than we deserve.

"Then my head will be exalted above the enemies who surround me" (verse 6). Is the psalmist gloating over the fact that his head is placed above his enemies? I do not think so. He is merely stating a fact, the fact that if we are on the Lord's side, our position is higher than anyone else's. We may think that truth is forever on the scaffold, but the time will come when truth will triumph gloriously and we with it, God willing.

"I will sing and make music to the Lord." The time of singing will surely come. Heaven will be the place where we sing the "Hallelujah Chorus." But even now we can sing in anticipation and in faith. The songs of David are to be sung even in this life. They are songs of confidence that we can sing in a world of bitter conflict because the outcome is already known.

Can you think of anything better than making music to the Lord? Perhaps we are not musically inclined, but we can always shout our praises. Let us hope that in the earth made new our voices will be carefully tuned and we can join the angels in making the vaults of heaven ring!

The Human Cry for Help

"Hear my voice when I call, O Lord" (verse 7). Faith can raise us to heights of ecstacy. But so long as we are in this world we cannot ignore its realities. The problems are real. Our weaknesses are evident. It is not long, therefore, before we raise our voices in prayer. Be merciful to us, we beg. Of course, we know that God is always merciful. But the prayer for mercy shows that we recognize our need.

"My heart says of you, 'Seek his face!' Your face, Lord, I will seek" (verse 8). The psalmist lets us know what is in his heart; he is blessed with a good conscience. The conscience can be a valuable asset. Some Gentiles had such consciences, which in-

dicated that they had the requirements of the law written in their hearts (see Romans 2:15). Unfortunately this is not the case with everyone. Some have corrupted consciences. "They claim to know God, but by their actions they deny him. They are detestable, disobedient and unfit for doing anything good" (Titus 1:15, 16).

The psalmist responds to the call of his heart immediately. He says: *"Your face, Lord, I will seek."* He then proceeds to ask the Lord not to hide His face from him (see verse 9). It is the human cry not to be forsaken, not to be rejected in anger. He knows what he deserves and pleads for mercy and God's presence.

Moses, the leader of Israel, felt the same need. He prayed: "If your Presence does not go with us, do not send us up from here." God graciously answered: "My Presence will go with you, and I will give you rest" (Exodus 33:14, 15). In the Hebrew the same word is used for *presence* and *face.*

In verse 10 the psalmist makes an interesting statement: *"Though my father and mother forsake me, the Lord will receive me."* Did he ever have his father or mother do this? I wonder how many young men have found comfort in this verse!

When I was a lad of about fifteen I remember realizing that one day I would have to leave the family nest and make my own way through the world. Not that my parents ever hinted at such a thing; I always felt welcome and loved at home. But I knew that I was growing up, and adulthood certainly meant wending my way through life independently. How would I manage it? Would I ever make it? It was then that I read this twenty-seventh psalm and latched onto the promise of verse 10. Then I was young, now I am old, and I can testify that God has never let me down.

"Teach me your way, O Lord" (verse 11). The psalmist recognized that he needed continued instruction. The time never comes when we no longer need to be taught. Teachers need to listen to God every day of their lives. The one who thinks he knows it all has not yet learned the very basics.

"Lead me in a straight path." The Muslim prays this prayer

from the Koran every time he bows toward Mecca. He knows that if he goes astray, the end is destruction. So it is for him, and so it is for us. Fortunately, God has not left us without guidance. Jesus said: "Enter through the narrow gate. For wide is the gate and broad is the road that leads to destruction, and many enter through it. But small is the gate and narrow the road that leads to life, and only a few find it" (Matthew 7:13, 14).

"Do not turn me over to the desire of my foes" (verse 12). The psalmist knows that the devil is ever ready to trip us up. He prays constantly, assured that God hears him and will not let him go. What a blessing to reach out the hand of faith and touch the hand of God. He is our Parent, and we His children can walk down life's pathway holding His hand. So long as we maintain that contact, we have no fear of failure.

The Secret of Success

"I am still confident of this: I will see the goodness of the Lord in the land of the living" (verse 13). From prayer the psalmist returns to a statement of confidence. The psalmist may have unanswered questions regarding many aspects of the world we live in. But of one thing he is confident: God is in control, and He has many followers. God is good, and many good people still live on this earth. We must not lose sight of the goal that God has for the world and for each one of us. We must answer one major question: In the conflict between good and evil, shall we be on God's side, or on the devil's side?

Finally comes that impressive word of advice: *"Wait on the Lord; be strong and take heart and wait for the Lord"* (verse 14).

Waiting, in this passage, means more than merely letting time pass by. It is the opposite from grumbling about delay. It is waiting in hope, waiting in eager expectation of the Lord's coming. It is making readiness for that coming the prime factor in our lives.

Waiting has rarely been easy. Sometimes we have to wait so that God can act. But we must always let *Him* take the initiative. Only by keeping in step with the Almighty can we be sure that we are accomplishing His purposes.

Chapter 10
The Burden of Sin: The Joy of Forgiveness

Psalm 32

The superscription ascribes this psalm to David, the man after God's own heart. It also tells us that it is a maskil. Scholars are not certain what this word means, but the margin of the NIV suggests: "Probably a literary or musical term." A plural form of this word, *maskillim*, is found in Daniel 12:3 and is there translated, "Those who are wise," or, in the margin, "who impart wisdom"—teachers. Thus we may expect this psalm to teach us something very important.

This psalm has traditionally been called a penitential psalm, and Martin Luther called it Pauline in its sentiment. We shall see why as we study it.

The Blessing of Forgiveness

"Blessed is he whose transgressions are forgiven, whose sins are covered" (verse 1). The first word of this psalm in Hebrew is *ashre*, a word meaning "blissfully happy" that we met in Psalm 1:1. When we say to someone, "God bless you," we are literally asking God to make him or her blissfully happy.

What is it that can make a person blissfully happy? It is the experience and knowledge of sins forgiven. Does it surprise you that David, the man after God's own heart, would be talking about sins forgiven? The Bible makes it clear that even devout men of God had their faults, so we must not be discouraged if we find ourselves failing repeatedly. Our attitude to the sin that we have committed matters more than the fact we have committed a sin.

We tend to have an idealized picture of David. We see him as a shepherd lad looking after his father's sheep. We know that he had the sterling qualities that made him a suitable candidate for kingship. We admire him as he goes forth to meet Goliath in the name of the Lord of Hosts. We marvel at his patience while Saul hunts him from pillar to post. Is this the person who writes a penitential psalm?

David was a young man of great promise, but he made some serious mistakes. We read about his sins of adultery and murder in 2 Samuel 11. If you were in David's shoes, would you excuse yourself by saying that you were subject to human frailty? Or would you seek to cover up the incident, perhaps with a bribe? Would you try to put the matter out of your mind, or attempt to make matters right by marrying the woman? This is what David did. But the Scripture says, "The thing David had done displeased the Lord" (verse 27).

God sent His prophet Nathan to rebuke the king. Nathan accomplished his task very tactfully. He began by telling the story of a rich man who had many sheep, and a poor man who had only one ewe lamb, but the ewe lamb was as dear to him as a daughter. Now the rich man needed to do some entertaining, but instead of taking one of his many sheep to slaughter, he took the ewe lamb.

The story angered David. He knew what it was like to care for sheep. He knew what a loss it would be for the poor man to lose his one ewe lamb. He wanted to have justice meted out, so he wanted to know who the guilty person was. Nathan replied: "You are the man!" (2 Samuel 12:7).

David was indeed guilty. Unknowingly he had condemned himself. David said, "I have sinned against the Lord," and immediately Nathan replied, "The Lord has taken away your sin" (verse 13). How quickly the Lord forgives! He is just waiting for us to repent and confess.

We tend to make a distinction between big sins and little sins. But sin is sin, and all sin brings separation between ourselves and God (see Isaiah 59:2). Cherishing willful and determined sin means that God cannot hear us, and without God, we are hopeless and helpless.

When the psalmist expresses the blessedness of one whose sins are forgiven, he is virtually saying that all have sinned. He is affirming what he stated in Psalm 14: "The Lord looks down from heaven on the sons of men to see if there are any who understand, any who seek God. All have turned aside, they have together become corrupt; there is no one who does good, not even one" (verses 2, 3).

You and I stand condemned before God. We can do nothing about our situation except to recognize it. Thank God, a plan has been laid down for our salvation. There is a way whereby we can be cleansed from sin.

In Romans 3:10-12 Paul quotes Psalm 14:1-3 and Psalm 53:1-3 as evidence that we are condemned as sinners. But he follows condemnation with hope: "Righteousness from God comes through faith in Jesus Christ to all who believe" (verse 22).

Paul refers to the experience of Abraham recorded in Genesis 15 as evidence to support this point. "Abraham believed God, and it was credited to him as righteousness" (Romans 4:3). In other words, Abraham was justified by faith, and not by works. Paul asserts that the words "it was credited to him as righteousness" were written, "not for [Abraham] alone, but also for us, to whom God will credit righteousness— for us who believe in him who raised Jesus our Lord from the dead" (Romans 4:22-24).

In describing his sin, the psalmist uses three Hebrew words:

1. *Pesha'*, usually translated "transgression," refers to the breaking of a law, which amounts to rebellion. David had broken the law when he committed adultery.

2. *Chattâ'âh*, a word which basically means a "missing of the mark," represents a deviation from a pathway marked out by God. David had certainly failed God in the responsibilities that had been placed on him as king. The greater the privileges, the greater the failure.

3. *'Avôn* refers to moral worthlessness, something crooked and twisted. Since the fall of Adam, our inherited nature is crooked and twisted. Only by the new birth can we be restored to communion and fellowship with God.

As David rejoices that his sins are forgiven, he uses three Hebrew words to describe what has happened to him:

1. *Nâsâ'*, meaning "to lift or carry away," shows that the sin is no longer there.

2. *Kâçâh* means "to cover, to put out of sight." When a sin is "covered," that sin no longer stands between us and God.

3. *Châshab* means "to charge with or impute to." When a person is no longer "charged" with a sin, his record is clear before God.

These two verses give threefold emphasis that David is forgiven: his act of rebellion is considered nonexistent; his deviation from the true pathway is not remembered; and his crookedness is not held against him. No wonder he is happy!

When sin is carried away, the barrier to communication between God and us is broken down. When sin is forgiven, the injured party, in this case God, does not hold anything against us. We can communicate as though nothing untoward had happened, for there is no anger, no resentment on God's part.

It is sin that alienates us from God. It is forgiveness that brings us into a right relationship with God. This reconciliation is wholly of God; we can do nothing to earn it or atone for it. When we repent of our sins, recognizing our crooked and twisted natures, and look to God, believing that He can and will help us, then our gracious God accomplishes for us what we can never accomplish for ourselves.

"In whose spirit is no deceit." The psalmist knows that he cannot hide anything from God. Why should he try? He is perfectly frank, perfectly honest in confessing his faults, his waywardness, and his rebellion. He does not excuse himself, nor does he rationalize his behavior.

The Burden and Pain of Sin

"When I kept silent" (verse 3). The psalmist did not confess his sin immediately. For a time he thought he would "get

away with it." But he soon found that his silence brought him only misery.

"My bones wasted away through my groaning all day long." Because bones are usually the last part of the body to decay, we see that David is not being literal here. This imagery suggests the extent that his spiritual condition affected physical well-being. Psychologists now recognize the close link between body and mind.

"For day and night your hand was heavy upon me; my strength was sapped as in the heat of summer" (verse 4). The knowledge that he had done wrong and displeased God weighed on David. The guilt and worry made him listless, distracted, and ineffective. Could the psalmist be more realistic in describing the distress and burden of sin? You and I can very well understand his feelings.

Confession and Relief

"Then I acknowledged my sin to you" (verse 5). David confessed his sin. But he did more than confess; he repented of his wrong. He acknowledged that he did not want anything to come between him and God, that his life and everything depended on God. Knowing that God had prospered him, he regretted that he had offended God by his sin and did not excuse himself.

David knew that it was against God that he had sinned, and therefore it was to God that he confessed his sin. Yet his confession had been open, because he had said to Nathan, "I have sinned," and no doubt word had gone out to the community. There is no shame in confessing our faults, but it may hurt our pride! The psalmist discovered that what the wise man says is true: "He who conceals his sins does not prosper, but whoever confesses and renounces them finds mercy" (Proverbs 28:13).

Of course, David knew that he would have to suffer the consequences of his sin. Nathan had said: "The Lord has taken away your sin. You are not going to die. But because by doing this you have made the enemies of the Lord show utter contempt, the son born to you will die" (2 Samuel 12:13, 14). And this prophecy was fulfilled. Furthermore, Absalom, David's son, conspired against his father, forcing David to flee from Jerusalem. But David proved his true repentance by accepting the events as they came, recognizing that they were permitted by God as a result of his sin.

"And did not cover up my iniquity. I said, 'I will confess my transgression to the Lord'—and you forgave the guilt of my sin." Note that the psalmist repeats the three words for *sin* that he used earlier in the psalm. Note also the repetition of the personal pronouns *I* and *my*. David does not try to hide his personal involvement or to minimize the enormity of his sin. No doubt he also remembered the character of God as revealed to Moses: "The Lord, the Lord, the compassionate and gracious God, slow to anger, abounding in love and faithfulness, maintaining love to thousands, and forgiving wickedness, rebellion and sin. Yet he does not leave the guilty unpunished" (Exodus 34:6, 7). God is supremely loving, but He is also absolutely just.

The psalmist now proceeds to give advice based on his experience. *"Therefore let everyone who is godly pray to you while you may be found"* (verse 6). Most likely the psalmist includes himself among the "godly" because they are not necessarily the perfect ones but the ones who have experienced God's grace. They are saints in the sense of being forgiven sinners who appreciate what God has done for them. We are blessed indeed if we can include ourselves in that category.

"While you may be found." This clause emphasizes that there is a day of grace, and we should make good use of our opportunities. The day may come when we shall seek repentance and not find it, or seek salvation after the doors of opportunity are closed. God is merciful and long-suffering, but the time will come when the door of mercy is closed, and those who have not made adequate preparation will find themselves outside the kingdom.

The prophet Isaiah gives similar advice. He says: "Seek the Lord while he may be found; call on him while he is near" (Isaiah 55:6). Jeremiah adds counsel from the Lord: "You will seek me and find me when you seek me with all your heart" (Jeremiah 29:13).

"Surely when the mighty waters rise, they will not reach him. You are my hiding place; you will protect me from trouble and surround me with songs of deliverance" (verses 6, 7). This is the prayer that the godly offer for promised deliverance in times of sudden crisis. They know the source of their help in times of danger. Their rejoicing with songs of deliverance reminds us of the songs that John the Revelator heard being sung in heaven (see Revelation 7:10, 12, 15-17).

God's Promises and Advice

"I will instruct you and teach you in the way you should go" (verse 8). God is always willing to give us counsel if we ask for it. Unfortunately, we often think we know the way and do not ask to be guided. Too confident in ourselves, we think that asking God for direction in the little details of our lives is not necessary. But in this regard we are mistaken; no matter is too small to be important or too little to be of consequence.

"I will counsel you and watch over you." What a blessing to have God's constant watchcare over us! Nothing can give us greater confidence than the knowledge that God is ever watching to guide our steps. With such guidance we have nothing to fear for the future, nothing to make us uncertain about the present, and nothing to regret about the past.

"Do not be like the horse or the mule, which have no understanding" (verse 9). We may smile as we read these words, along with a similar warning from the wise man: "A whip for the horse, a halter for the donkey, and a rod for the backs of fools" (Proverbs 26:3). While we may wish to exclude ourselves from any of these categories, we should remember that we, like David, are sometimes stubborn in the way we react to counsel and advice. While we smile, let us take the counsel to heart and be men and women of understanding.

"But must be controlled by bit and bridle or they will not come to you." One summer I had the privilege of spending a few weeks with my grandparents in North Ireland. My grandfather owned a farm and had a horse called Charlie. Charlie had a mind of his own. If he saw my grandfather at the gate, he knew what was coming next and would not let my

grandfather come near him. So my grandfather used a ruse; he would carry a bag of oats in front of him, and Charlie would put his nose into the bag. A moment was all that Grandpa needed. In a trice he had the bridle over Charlie's head, and, willy-nilly, Charlie had to go where Grandpa directed him.

The Joy of a Restored Relationship

"Many are the woes of the wicked, but the Lord's unfailing love surrounds the man who trusts in him" (verse 10). David well knew that the woes of the wicked are not always external; more often than not they are internal. David knew from experience that one cannot have peace and rest while living contrary to God's commands. Sin and a refusal to confess one's sin leads only to dissatisfaction, discouragement, and a fearful looking forward to the day of judgment. The psalmist learned this lesson and was ready to give his testimony to others.

What a blessing to have a God of love, One who understands our weaknesses and failings, One who will do all He can to help us. We can always turn to Him in our need, and He will never fail the trust we have in Him.

"Rejoice in the Lord and be glad, you righteous; sing, all you who are upright in heart!" (verse 11). This verse applies to every one of us. We all sincerely want to be upright. We all seek to do what is right. We all recognize the love of God and the provision He has made for our salvation. What more do we need to cause us to rejoice and sing?

Chapter 11
Living Wisely in a Wicked World
Psalm 37

In Hebrew this psalm is an acrostic; every stanza in the poem begins with the successive letter of the Hebrew alphabet. Perhaps the acrostic was a mnemonic to help the students memorize the psalm. Obviously in a long psalm, this one a string of proverbs, an interesting device will help students remember the principles outlined as a guide to life.

Thus this psalm differs from the others we have studied in that it does not record the experiences of the psalmist and God's response to them. Rather, it contains a set of rules that will enable us to pick our way through life and make proper choices. Furthermore, the psalmist gives us reasons for the rules he includes. He rightly assumes that we want to know why one course of conduct may be better than another. The psalm has been described as a psalm of recompense and retribution.

This psalm addresses a question we often ask: Why do the wicked seem to prosper and the righteous have a hard time? We reason that if God is good, and we believe He is, then He should protect His followers and let the wicked reap the consequences of their wickedness. The psalmist does not deny that we are living in a topsy-turvy world. He recognizes the existence of many situations we cannot fully understand. But he gives us some good advice.

Relating to the Evil We See

"Do not fret because of evil men or be envious of those who

99

do wrong" (verse 1). The Hebrew word for "do not fret" is a word that suggests heat. Literally the word means, "do not get inflamed." In colloquial English we would say, "Don't get hot under the collar!"

This good advice is not easy to follow, especially for those of us who lose our tempers rather easily. We want to undertake a crusade against evildoers; we want to be sure that they do not get away with their wicked schemes. The psalmist says: Do not let the immediate situation upset you. Bide your time as God bides His. Everything will work out right in the end.

Why should we bide our time? Because *"like the grass they will soon wither, like green plants they will soon die away."* In other words, the time will come soon enough when the wicked will reap the just reward of their deeds. Be patient. Let God work out His plan. You and I do not have the wisdom to handle situations as they need to be handled. Let God do that. We need to keep our hands off matters that are not our business.

"The wicked plot against the righteous and gnash their teeth at them" (verse 12). Obviously the wicked are the enemies of the righteous. They seek to undermine their activities. Gnashing or grinding teeth suggests their deep enmity. How does God respond to this?

"The Lord laughs at the wicked, for he knows their day is coming" (verse 13). Retribution does not necessarily come immediately. The wicked think that they can do what they like with impunity. They arrogantly attack God's people and think that they will get away with it. God responds with laughter at the incongruity of the situation. Wrong cannot forever sit on the throne. With God in control, the time will come when everyone receives the just reward of his action. The wicked may think that their plots are succeeding very well, but they will soon learn differently.

"The wicked borrow and do not repay" (verse 21). The wicked have little sense of responsibility. They do not recognize their obligation to pay back their debts. Society cannot function properly unless each member lives up to promises made.

"The wicked lie in wait for the righteous, seeking their very

lives; but the Lord will not leave them in their power or let them be condemned when brought to trial" (verses 32, 33).

An outstanding example of this protection is the life of Jesus. The authorities tried their best to seize Him, but they could not do anything till His time had come. On the cross they thought they had achieved a signal victory, but the supposed victory proved to be a resounding defeat. The psalmist does not say that the righteous will never fall into the hands of the wicked, but he does say that the Lord will not *leave* them there. It is not the immediate situation that counts; it is the final outcome.

Putting Our Trust in God

"Trust in the Lord and do good; dwell in the land and enjoy safe pasture" (verse 3). The Hebrew word used here for *trust*, *bâtach*, means "enjoy the security that comes from knowing that your confidence is well placed." We may be sure that when we place our affairs in God's hands, they are perfectly safe. Furthermore, when we know that God is in control, we do not have to worry about the events that take place around us. Even though it may seem that events are going in the wrong direction, we need not be concerned because everything is in God's hands.

"Trust in God" is a fine motto. But how often we find people trusting more in money, in their supposed superior intelligence, or in their preparations for defense. Trust in God is a relationship with God that is worth more than anything else in this world.

"Do good." The life of trust in God is not a life of inactivity; it is not leaving everything for God to do. We must carry out our God-given responsibilities faithfully. We are partners with God; when we do our part, God will do His. The psalmist is anxious that we are not discouraged from doing good because of the evil around us. Jesus went about "doing good," regardless of the way people treated Him and the injustices He saw. We can spend our lives in no better way than in following in the footsteps of the Master.

"Dwell in the land and enjoy safe pasture." This suggests

that the Christian should live at peace with all people. Even with other church members, he may have to exert himself to live at peace (see 1 Thessalonians 5:13). Maintaining peace and harmony may not be easy, but Christians strive to avoid conflict whenever possible.

Enjoying *"safe pasture"* is also a privilege we may have. Some Christians struggle under difficult circumstances, but the majority of North American Christians live relatively comfortable lives. Do we appreciate what God has provided? Do we recognize the source of blessing and show our gratitude to God for what He has done?

"Delight yourself in the Lord and he will give you the desires of your heart" (verse 4). The Hebrew word here means "take exquisite delight!" The Jerusalem Bible says: "Make Jahweh your only joy." We have many things to delight us in the world, but God should be the object of our supreme delight. Note the consequences of such an experience with God: He will give us the desires of our heart, those innermost and deepest desires, which, when fulfilled, leave us saying: "We have nothing more to ask of God. He has satisfied us to the full."

"Commit your way to the Lord; trust in him and he will do this" (verse 5). The Hebrew used here literally means, "Roll your way upon Yahweh"; that is, turn everything you have over to Him. Evidently the psalmist is not thinking of any half measures. In this absolute commitment we keep nothing back from God. He has all we are, all we hope to be. You and I can meet that high standard of dedication only as God Himself makes it possible in our lives. Of ourselves we can do nothing except to choose such a commitment. Thank God for the desire we have in our hearts to do God's will, which God Himself will bring to pass.

"Be still before the Lord and wait patiently for him" (verse 7). "Be still" literally means "be silent." Do we talk too much to God? Perhaps we should spend more times in silence, so as to hear God's voice speaking to us. Perhaps we are worried about everything that is happening around us, and we babble away to God! The second half of this verse says, *"Do not fret when*

men succeed in their ways, when they carry out their wicked schemes." This suggests the areas beyond the legitimate scope of our concern. Some things we cannot change. In such cases let God work. Continuing to talk about some matters accomplishes nothing. In such cases "silence is golden." Happy are we when we can "let go and let God."

A secret of success in the Christian life is in waiting "patiently for him." In our hurry, we sometimes go ahead of God—with disastrous results. God is not slow, either in His second coming or in answering our prayers. We need to learn how to wait in hope, realizing that our impatience does not alter God's timetable.

"The meek will inherit the land and enjoy great peace" (verse 11). These words immediately remind us of the Sermon on the Mount. Perhaps Jesus had this psalm in mind as He taught the multitude (see Matthew 5:5). Commenting on the thought of meekness, an inspired Christian writer has said:

> The difficulties we have to encounter may be very much lessened by that meekness which hides itself in Christ. If we possess the humility of our Master, we shall rise above the slights, the rebuffs, the annoyances, to which we are daily exposed, and they will cease to cast a gloom over the spirit. The highest evidence of nobility in a Christian is self-control. He who under abuse or cruelty fails to maintain a calm and trustful spirit robs God of His right to reveal in him His own perfection of character. Lowliness of heart is the strength that gives victory to the followers of Christ; it is the token of their connection with the courts above (*The Desire of Ages*, p. 301).

The End Results of Doing Evil

"Like the grass they will soon wither, like green plants they will soon die away" (verse 2). When Jesus spoke of "grass of the field, which is here today, and tomorrow is thrown into the fire" (see Matthew 6:30; Luke 12:28), He spoke of something very transitory. By contrast, you and I are sustained by God,

since we follow the injunction of the Master to "seek first his kingdom and his righteousness" (Matthew 6:30). Because the wicked do not seek God's kingdom, their existence is as transitory as the grass, as green plants that have no water and wither away.

"*Evil men will be cut off, but those who hope in the Lord will inherit the land*" (verse 9). The contrast here is between inheriting the land, having something in the future, and being "cut off," being nothing! What a dismal future is in store for the wicked person! If this life is the only one we have, some people would say it is hardly worth living. Certainly it is not in God's plan that you and I should have no existence beyond this one.

The psalmist makes sure that we have not misunderstood him as to the fate of the wicked. He repeats the expression "*cut off*" in verses 22, 28, 34, and 38. He uses the expression "*vanish like smoke*" (verse 20) to indicate a total disappearance, and "*destroyed*" (verse 38) to determine an act of annihilation. Then he adds, "*Though you look for them, they will not be found*" (verse 10). Just in case we should think that the fate of a person who had all that this world could offer him was different from that of any other wicked person, he gives this personal testimony: "*I have seen a wicked and ruthless man flourishing like a green tree in its native soil, but he soon passed away and was no more; though I looked for him, he could not be found*" (verses 35, 36).

Finally, the psalmist tells us how the activities of the wicked can backfire. "*The wicked draw the sword and bend the bow to bring down the poor and needy, to slay those whose ways are upright. But their swords will pierce their own hearts, and their bows will be broken*" (verses 14, 15). A fuller picture of the complete destruction of the wicked is found in Revelation 20:1, 2, 14, 15. It is for you and me to choose the kind of fate we would like for ourselves, and then it is for us to choose the way we shall live while here on earth.

The Lasting Joys of Doing Good

By way of review we may note that God will give the

righteous *"the desires of [their] heart"* (verse 4). He will give them *"the land,"* and they will *"enjoy great peace"* (verse 11). What is the principle behind their contentment? *"Better the little that the righteous have than the wealth of many wicked"* (verse 16). Those who decide to serve God are promised that their needs—but not necessarily great wealth—will be provided. If they have more than they need, they have the opportunity of helping those who are less fortunate.

Some people are wealthy because God has blessed them. Others are wealthy because they are greedy. They amass wealth, supposing that wealth will give them happiness and security. They find, often too late, that happiness is not found in wealth, nor security in riches. Wealth may cause anxiety, which often breeds ill health. So what have they gained?

Jesus told His disciples, "I tell you the truth, it is hard for a rich man to enter the kingdom of heaven." He made this statement after a rich young man came to Jesus, asking what he should do to inherit eternal life. Jesus told him to sell what he had and give to the poor and have treasure in heaven. The young man left Jesus sadly, because, we are told, "he had great wealth" (see Matthew 19:16-24).

Another theme in this psalm is that a person needs some power outside of himself if he is truly to do what is right. *"The Lord delights in the way of the man whose steps he has made firm; though he stumble, he will not fall, for the Lord upholds him with his hand"* (verses 23, 24). Salvation does not result from what we do for ourselves, but what God has done for us. Mrs. White has said: "Salvation does not come through our seeking after God but through God's seeking after us" (*Christ's Object Lessons*, p. 189). Paul said to the Philippians: "It is God who works in you to will and to act according to his good purpose" (Philippians 2:13). The psalmist points out that God is interested in everyone who wants to do His will. God makes the steps of such a person firm. If such a person should stumble—and do we not all?—God stretches out a loving arm to uphold him or her. What an assurance this is! What a blessing! God will guide us and keep us. In His strength we can walk right into the kingdom by His grace.

Chapter 12
God, Our Refuge and Strength

Psalm 46

Unlike the psalms we have been studying so far, this psalm is not attributed to David, but to the sons of Korah. Martin Luther based his hymn "Ein' Feste Burg" on this psalm, a hymn that came to be called "The battle hymn of the Reformation." Luther's hymn is not a translation of the psalm, but Luther applies the truth of the first verse when he says: "Did we in our own strength confide, / Our striving would be losing." And again, "We will not fear, for God hath willed / His truth to triumph through us." May that be true in our own experience!

It is said that, whenever the going was hard, Luther would say to his colleague, Melanchthon, "Come, Philip, let us sing the forty-sixth psalm." This psalm can give courage in times of stress. Sometimes it may seem to us, as it did to Luther, that this world is "with devils filled," who "threaten to undo us," but with God on our side we have nothing to fear.

Our Refuge and Strength

It is noteworthy that the psalm begins and ends with God. This is how it ought to be with us. The ideal life begins with a recognition of God as the One upon whom we can depend at all times, and ends with the testimony that God has been with us throughout our lives to guide us and provide our every need.

Our refuge is not a place; it is a Person. When we go to

Him, He enfolds us in His arms. He communicates with us and we with Him. The personal touch is much more precious than the impersonality of a place. Furthermore, God is accessible everywhere. He is here, right where we are. We have immediate recourse to Him in time of need.

The children of Israel had a system whereby anyone who had unwittingly caused the death of a person could flee to a city of refuge. Designated cities were so located that no one had to flee more than a half-day's journey. But even that short journey involved risk; so long as the person was outside the city, he could be the victim of the avenger of blood (see Numbers 35:9-28).

Ellen G. White makes the following application to the Christian:

> The sinner is exposed to eternal death, until he finds a hiding place in Christ; and as loitering and carelessness might rob the fugitive of his only chance of life, so delays and indifference may prove the ruin of the soul. Satan, the great adversary, is on the track of every transgressor of God's holy law, and he who is not sensible of his danger, and does not earnestly seek shelter in the eternal refuge, will fall prey to the destroyer (*Patriarchs and Prophets*, p. 517).

"God is our refuge and strength, an ever present help in trouble" (verse 1). The idea of a refuge is only one of the figures of speech used to characterize God. We may be familiar with another image, that of a Rock, expressed in verse in Toplady's well-known hymn: "Rock of Ages, cleft for me, / Let me hide myself in Thee."

God is not our refuge in the sense that we go to Him as a last resort; we need God's protection every minute of our lives. We are wise if we recognize that many times in the battle for truth we need to invoke God's protection. Knowing that He is always available reassures us.

Soldiers must have a home base, a place to go for recuperation and supplies. God is the Christians' home base—a home base available to us as needed.

Soldiers need strength to endure in the battle. God is the Christians' strength, enabling us to fight temptations and overcome them. Merely fleeing from danger is not enough. We must be able to fight the evil one and defeat him. Here is where God gives us strength.

Our graduating class of 1931 at Stanborough Park College in England chose as its motto the words of a hymn by Edward Turney:

> I will go in the strength of the Lord,
> In the path He hath mark'd for my feet;
> I will follow the light of His Word!
> Nor shrink from the dangers I meet.

The fourth stanza says:

> I will go in the strength of the Lord
> To each conflict which faith may require;
> And His grace, as my shield and reward,
> My courage and zeal shall inspire.

I have always been proud of those words and prayed that they might express my experience. God is my refuge and strength, for which I am truly thankful.

"*An ever present help in trouble.*" In the story of Hezekiah, King of Judah, we learn that the king received a threatening message from his enemy. What did he do? He "went up to the temple of the Lord and spread it out before the Lord" (2 Kings 19:14). "That night the angel of the Lord went out and put to death a hundred and eighty-five thousand men in the Assyrian camp" (verse 35). It was God who saved Hezekiah out of all his troubles. We are not surprised to read that Hezekiah "trusted in the Lord, the God of Israel. . . . He held fast to the Lord and did not cease to follow him; he kept the commands the Lord had given Moses. And the Lord was with him; he was successful in whatever he undertook" (2 Kings 18:5-7).

"*Therefore we will not fear, though the earth give way and the mountains fall into the heart of the sea, though its waters roar and foam and the mountains quake with their surging"* (verses 2, 3). This verse describes events in nature that would normally terrify us. If you have been in an earthquake and have felt the motion of the earth beneath you, then you know how helpless one can feel. We generally think of the ground beneath us as solid, but when that solidity disappears, to what can we cling? If a mountain starts moving, who are we to stop it?

Have you been out on the sea and seen water from horizon to horizon? Have you stood by Niagara Falls and seen the mighty rush of water? Water's power and potential for destruction is frightening. We need to remember the One who created earth and mountains and seas and all the forces of nature. If we are in His hands, we have nothing to fear.

The River and a City

"There is a river whose streams make glad the city of God, the holy place where the Most High dwells" (verse 4). In this section the psalmist changes the imagery completely. Instead of waters that "roar and foam," we have a river that flows gently by. Instead of mountains falling into the sea, we have a city of comparative peace. What do these symbols mean? What is the psalmist trying to tell us?

1. A river is a source of life to a community. Egypt would not exist as a nation if it were not for the Nile that flows through it from south to north. Babylon would not have reached its stage of fortune if it had not been for the Euphrates that gave drink to the thirsty and water to the land. The same can be said for Rome on the Tiber and London on the Thames.

2. Isaiah the prophet gives the following message to Israel: "I will pour water on the thirsty land, and streams on the dry ground; I will pour out my Spirit on your offspring, and my blessing on your descendants" (Isaiah 44:3). Water can be a symbol of God's blessing, both physical and spiritual.

3. Jesus said to Nicodemus: "I tell you the truth, unless a man is born of water and the Spirit, he cannot enter the

kingdom of God" (John 3:5). To the woman of Samaria, He said: "Everyone who drinks this water will be thirsty again, but whoever drinks the water I give him will never thirst. Indeed, the water I give him will become in him a spring of water welling up to eternal life" (John 4:13, 14). Water is a symbol of cleansing; it is a symbol of eternal life. When we drink of the water of life, a gift that God provides, our thirst for salvation is quenched.

The presence of water, then, has a spiritual as well as a physical meaning. Just as we cannot live without physical water for more than a few days, so we cannot truly live without the spiritual refreshing that only God can give.

What about the city? Does the psalmist have a particular city in mind? First let us note the following characteristics:

1. A city represents a dwelling place of people. It can be a place of safety because of its surrounding walls and gates. Unfortunately, it can be a center of wickedness too. According to Scripture, Cain was the first person to build a city (see Genesis 4:17). After the Flood, the people said: "Come, let us build ourselves a city" (Genesis 11:4). Genesis tells about other wicked cities—Sodom and Gomorrah. But cities are not necessarily places of wickedness. The book of Revelation tells us of a city that comes down out of heaven from God (see Revelation 21:10).

2. Did the psalmist have in mind the city of Jerusalem, the city of David, where the temple was located? The trouble with this identification is that no river runs through Jerusalem. Hezekiah did channel spring water into the city by a tunnel, which may be seen to this day (see 2 Kings 20:20). Jerusalem was fortunate to have such a spring, but today it depends on rain water and water that is piped in from distant sources.

3. The psalmist specifically refers to a "city of God," a city in which God is worshiped. Such a city is described as "the bride, the wife of the Lamb" (Revelation 21:9). It has a "river of the water of life, as clear as crystal, flowing from the throne of God and of the Lamb down the middle of the great street of the city" (Revelation 22:1, 2). Surely the psalmist has in mind an ideal city, but a real place nevertheless. Abraham was look-

ing forward to just such a city, "whose architect and builder is God" (Hebrews 11:10).

The relationship of the river to the city is that one "makes glad" the other. In God's ideal universe everything is interconnected to bring joy and happiness. It is sin that has brought about disharmony and friction. The psalmist looks forward to the time when proper relationships will be restored, resulting in joy and peace.

The connection between the first and second parts of the psalm is that in the first we have a picture of man living in a world of turmoil. In the second, thanks to God's provision, man can live at peace with God and his fellowmen. The secret of this relationship is that *"God is within her."* We can enjoy the fruits of the Spirit, which are "love, joy, peace, patience, kindness, goodness, faithfulness, gentleness and self-control" (Galatians 5:22, 23).

What a blessing that the city *"will not fall"* (verse 5). God's promises are sure. His assurances are as strong as a rock. When God says He is preparing a city, when Jesus says He is preparing a place for you and me (see John 14:2), we have a piece of the rock. It will not fail or fall.

"God will help her at break of day" (verse 5). God has a timetable that He is working out. The wise man has said, "There is a time for everything" (Ecclesiastes 3:1). We tend to be in a hurry. We want things done quickly. We must learn to be patient and wait in hope. When I was young I expected Jesus to come during my lifetime. So did my father expect the second coming during his lifetime. We have pointed to the signs of Christ's coming and said, "Any time now!" Yet Jesus has not come. Some speak of this delay as a tragedy. Is it really so? Peter sets our thinking straight when he says: "The Lord is not slow in keeping his promise, as some understand slowness. He is patient with you, not wanting anyone to perish, but everyone to come to repentance" (2 Peter 3:9).

Safety in Times of Trouble

"Nations are in uproar, kingdoms fall" (verse 6). Here we have a vivid picture of the times in which we live. Nations

compete for power, for trade. They are suspicious of one another and spend millions on self-defense. Yet some rise and others fall. All this anxiety and feverish activity need not cause us concern; our God is in control. In His good time He will put an end to evil and establish His everlasting kingdom of peace and righteousness. Yes, we agree with the psalmist when he says: *"The Lord Almighty is with us; the God of Jacob is our fortress"* (verse 7).

Note how God calls Himself the God of Jacob. Speaking to Moses out of the burning bush, God said: "I am the God of your father, the God of Abraham, the God of Isaac and the God of Jacob" (Exodus 3:6). Abraham was the father of the faithful, and God is the Father of the faithful; Isaac was the son of promise, and God is the God of those who are born again. But God is also the God of Jacob, the supplanter, the one who deceived his father and robbed his older brother of the birthright, the one who had noble goals, but used devious means to achieve them. God is not only the God of the noble; He is also the God of all sinners—if only we will accept Him.

"He lifts his voice, the earth melts." Nothing can stand in the way of the Lord. All nature bows before Him. We cannot begin to imagine God's most formidable power. But the important fact for us to understand is that "the Lord Almighty is with us; the God of Jacob is our fortress" (verse 7). Notice the words *with us* and *our*; they are key words in our relationship with God.

Come, and See!

God always treats us as rational beings, whether we deserve the categorization or not! It is our privilege to see for ourselves, to come to our own conclusions.

"Come and see the works of the Lord, the desolations he has brought on the earth" (verse 8). We are invited to see how God has intervened in human history. Unfortunately, our vision may often be limited to what man has done. Ellen White has identified a true understanding of history in the following words:

> In the annals of human history the growth of na-
> tions, the rise and fall of empires, appear as depend-
> ent on the will and prowess of man. The shaping of
> events seems, to a great degree, to be determined by
> his power, ambition, or caprice. But in the word of God
> the curtain is drawn aside, and we behold, behind,
> above, and through all the play and counterplay of
> human interests and power and passions, the agencies
> of the all-merciful One, silently, patiently working out
> the counsels of His own will (*Education*, p. 173).

Is this what we see in history and the events around us?
God permits evil men to accomplish their purposes sometimes,
and so we may see desolation, destruction, and carnage. The
results of sin that we see make us hate sin and the author of
sin and thus turn to God. At other times, God *"makes wars
cease"* (verse 8). *"He breaks the bow and shatters the spear, he
burns the shields with fire"* (verse 9). A time will come when
the horror of evil no longer turns people to God. God therefore
puts an end to it. Are we not all looking forward to that time
when sin and persistent sinners will be destroyed? "Amen.
Come, Lord Jesus" (Revelation 22:20).

Be Still and Know

"Be still, and know that I am God" (verse 10). There comes
a time in a turbulent world when God says, "Enough! Be
quiet!" God cannot allow us to continue rushing from one
thing to another. We must pause and consider our ways. The
command is as authoritative as the command of Jesus on the
Sea of Galilee, "Quiet! Be still!" (Mark 4:39). The wind died
down, and there was complete calm.

When all is said and done, we must acknowledge that God
is God. We may not see Him, but He is there. We may not be
aware of Him, but He is present. We may think that few
people pay any attention to God, but God says: *"I will be exalted among the nations, I will be exalted in the earth"* (verse
10). Happy are we if we know that God is God, that He is in
control! Happy are we when we can keep calm in troubled

times, knowing that such times will not last forever. Some matters take time to work out, but God moves inexorably forward. We may keep our affairs completely in His hands, knowing that God will do "immeasurably more than all we ask or imagine, according to his power that is at work within us" (Ephesians 3:20). And so we say with Paul, "To him be glory in the church and in Christ Jesus throughout all generations, for ever and ever! Amen" (verse 21).

The psalmist ends his psalm with the glorious words: *"The Lord Almighty is with us; the God of Jacob is our fortress"* (verse 11). To this truth we cling; to this truth we pin our hopes.

As we ponder the promise relayed by the psalmist, let us with courage press on with our assigned duties. "We have nothing to fear for the future, except as we shall forget the way the Lord has led us, and His teaching in our past history" (*Life Sketches*, p. 196).

Chapter 13
Rejoicing in God's World

Psalm 66

The theme of the psalm is rejoicing because we live in God's world. It emphasizes our need to praise God for the great power He exercises on our behalf. Interestingly, Ellen White tells us that Jesus often sang this psalm.

Shouting to God for Joy

"Shout with joy to God, all the earth!" (verse 1). The psalmist assumes the role of a leader in a praise service. "Let me hear your voices ring for joy" is his message. But the psalmist's appeal is not limited to those who attend church; he addresses "all the earth." Every man, woman, and child is called upon to *"shout with joy to God."* Do we hear the call?

In a church service where, presumably, it may be deemed proper to shout to God, do we ever raise our voices in acclamation? Even in hymn singing, when we can surely sing out, do we raise our voices beyond a whisper? Why do we hesitate to let our voices be heard? Perhaps it is a matter of our training in church decorum. We feel that in the presence of God we should be quiet. In many churches even the architecture seems to say, "Hush! We are in the presence of God and should keep silence."

Whether we think we ought to express our feelings exuberantly in church is less important than asking ourselves whether we have feelings of joy to express. We need to be sure that we are well enough acquainted with God and His goodness to us that we can shout to God with joy when circumstances are appropriate.

The church in our day has been described as "lukewarm" (see Revelation 3:16). It is neither "cold," lacking in feeling, nor "hot," abounding in spiritual energy. Can it be that prayer has become a form, that church service is a ceremony, that Christian duties are humdrum? Does the mission appeal fall on deaf ears? Has the mission story lost its excitement? Do we make out our checks to the church as a matter of routine or fail to do so when the budget is tight? Do we think that it is for others to respond to the calls for help? Do we have nothing to shout about, except our grumbles and complaints? Listen to the psalmist:

"Sing to the glory of his name; offer him glory and praise!" (verse 2). God's name is His character. His glory is manifested in all His works. When we sing to the glory of His name, we extol His goodness, we praise Him for all that He has done. This favorite hymn is an example of a modern song of praise.

> For the beauty of the earth,
> For the glory of the skies,
> For the love which from our birth
> Over and around us lies,
> Lord of all, to Thee we raise
> This our grateful song of praise.

We offer God glory and praise when we are appreciative of all His gifts, when we recognize that He is the Creator and Sustainer. Ellen White says: "Look at the wonderful and beautiful things of nature. Think of their marvelous adaptation to the needs and happiness, not only of man, but of all living creatures. The sunshine and the rain, that gladden and refresh the earth, the hills and seas and plains, all speak to us of the Creator's love" (*Steps to Christ*, p. 9).

"Say to God, 'How awesome are your deeds!'" (verse 3). Just in case we do not know what to say, the psalmist puts words in our mouth. *Awesome.* God's deeds are awesome in the sense that they strike one with wonder and fear. (NEB uses the

word *fearful.*) This fear is awe, not terror. We stand in awe before the wonders of God's creation.

We need to be aware of God's greatness and always come into His presence in a spirit of reverence and awe. Perhaps Isaac Watts's hymn is popular for the way it expresses this awe and respect.

> Before Jehovah's awful throne,
> Ye nations, bow with sacred joy;
> Know that the Lord is God alone;
> He can create, and He destroy.

"*So great is your power that your enemies cringe before you.*" The Hebrew word translated "cringe" here suggests either that the enemies pay only feigned homage, or that they are cut down to size, their arrogance gone. In either case, they refuse to acknowledge God's true greatness. How different it is with God's people, who acknowledge God for what He truly is.

"*All the earth bows down to you; they sing praise to you, they sing praise to your name*" (verse 4). That is why John the Revelator can say he saw a group on the sea of glass, singing the song of Moses and the Lamb:

> Great and marvelous are your deeds,
>   Lord God Almighty.
> Just and true are your ways,
>   King of the ages.
> Who will not fear you, O Lord,
>   and bring glory to your name?
> For you alone are holy.
> All nations will come
>   and worship before you,
> for your righteous acts have been
>   revealed (Revelation 15:3, 4).

Gratitude to the God of History

"*Come and see what God has done, how awesome his works in man's behalf!*" (verse 5). What God has done in creation is certainly wonderful, but what God continually does on behalf of people is awesome. The psalmist now directs our attention to the way that God has guided and provided in history.

If you were asked to describe an event in history that revealed God's marvelous power, what event would you cite? Would you turn to an event in biblical history recorded in Joshua 10:10-14? The remarkable story says that "the Lord hurled large hailstones down on [the enemy] from the sky, and more of them died from the hailstones than were killed by the swords of the Israelites" (verse 11). How remarkable that the hailstones should so fall as to destroy only the enemy!

Furthermore, "the sun stopped in the middle of the sky and delayed going down about a full day" (verse 13). Knowing what we know now about astronomy and the revolution of the earth on its own axis, such a miracle is unimaginable. Mrs. White comments on the incident as follows:

> The Spirit of God inspired Joshua's prayer, that evidence might again be given of the power of Israel's God. Hence the request did not show presumption on the part of the great leader. . . . He did all that human energy could do, and then he cried in faith for divine aid. The secret of success is the union of divine power with human effort. Those who achieve the greatest results are those who rely implicitly upon the Almighty Arm. . . . The men of prayer are the men of power (*Patriarchs and Prophets*, p. 509).

For the Christian, the greatest event in history is the birth, death, and resurrection of our Lord. Here we see God's supreme action on behalf of humanity. The cross, which might seem to be a symbol of shame, was rather a sign of victory, so that Paul could say: "May I never boast except in the cross of our Lord Jesus Christ" (Galatians 6:14). The resurrection came as a surprise to the disciples, who had never really paid attention to the words of Jesus (see Matthew 20:19; Mark 9:31; 10:34; Luke 18:33; 24:7). But after the resurrection and ascension and Pentecost, they had a message that would turn the world upside down!

"He turned the sea into dry land, they passed through the river on foot—come, let us rejoice in him" (verse 6). The psalmist refers to two events in the history of the children of Israel in which God showed His mighty power through spectacular miracles. One was the crossing of the Red Sea; the other was the crossing of the river Jordan.

In the twentieth century miracles are often the butt of scientific scorn. But the Christian cannot understand the Bible without recognizing fully a transcendent God who not only brought the universe into existence, but who also takes a continuing interest in human history and has often intervened on behalf of His people. Because God actively intervenes in history, the psalmist calls us to rejoice in Him. We are not left alone in this world to fend for ourselves; we have a God who will come to our aid whenever we ask Him and need Him.

"He rules forever by his power, his eyes watch the nations— let not the rebellious rise up against him" (verse 7). The psalmist issues a warning against anyone who supposes he can resist God's power. Some truths we can never deny—and one is the futility of resistance to an omnipotent God. Such denial is also foolish, because God's omnipotence is usually used for man's benefit. Why deny the good, the power from which all blessings flow? C. H. Spurgeon sums up this verse well: God "oversees all and overlooks none."

The Blessing of God in Our Lives

"Praise our God, O peoples, let the sound of his praise be heard; he has preserved our lives and kept our feet from slipping" (verses 8, 9). The Hebrew word *bârak* is here translated "praise." When translated "bless" and used in the context of blessing God, it means "adore on bended knee." People who bless God recognize that God is gracious and faithful, and on bended knee they praise God for His goodness and love.

The psalmist urges that the sound of praise to God be heard. Praising God is not something we do in secret, but neither should it be a selfish praise, as exhibited by some Pharisees in the New Testament times. We are free to express our praise to God for His many mercies, letting our neighbors and family friends know how we appreciate the source of blessings. Our children will also be aware in our lives how we owe everything to God.

"He has preserved our lives and kept our feet from slipping" (verse 9). Some see the fulfillment of this promise when they recover from serious illness or escape a dreadful calamity. Most Christians recognize that God has a plan for our lives, and we are anxious to fulfill that plan (see Jeremiah 1:5). We have no greater privilege than that of accomplishing God's purpose for our lives.

What a blessing it is to know that God keeps our feet from slipping. We watch our small children carefully to protect them from falling. When they do fall, we pick them up and set them on their feet again. That is what God does for us. We all make mistakes, but when we recognize our faults and ask God to forgive us, He does so immediately. John puts it very beautifully: "If we confess our sins, he is faithful and just and will forgive us our sins and purify us from all unrighteousness" (1 John 1:9). I like that extra step God takes; He cleanses us from the confessed sin and makes sure we are cleansed from *all* unrighteousness.

"For you, O God, tested us; you refined us like silver" (verse 10). God gives us freedom to choose, and with that freedom comes a test. God placed in the Garden of Eden a tree of knowledge of good and evil and told Adam and Eve not to eat its fruit. Some people think that if God had not placed that tree in the garden, there would have been no sin. But without opportunity to choose obedience or disobedience, human beings would have been like robots. This is far from God's intention for you and me. Obedience by choice is preferable to mechanized or forced obedience. God wants you and me to serve Him freely, joyously. Only then can we reflect the image in which we were originally created.

To illustrate the way God makes us what we ought to be, the psalmist uses the imagery of refining silver. The ore, with all its impurities, is heated until all the dross is separated, leaving the valuable pure silver. Similarly, God places us in varying circumstances that test our choice, that test our endurance, that help us overcome our weaknesses. The process is not easy, but the result is satisfying, both to ourselves and to God. God wants us to be the very best that we can be. Is that not our goal too?

"You brought us into prison and laid burdens on our backs" (verse 11). But sometimes we bring punishment upon ourselves, and God permits it to teach us lessons. Discipline is never pleasant to take, but can bring salutary results.

The burdens on our backs are a means of increasing strength and usefulness. Paul instructs us to "carry each other's burdens," and then he adds, "Each one should carry his own load" (Galatians 6:2, 5). Life involves service, and just as pack animals are expected to carry loads according to their capacity, so we are expected to shoulder our responsibilities according to our age, experience, and abilities. God gives us burdens to carry, and in carrying them without complaining we show our love and devotion to Him.

"You let men ride over our heads; we went through fire and water" (verse 12). Riding over someone's head seems to be the ultimate indignity, yet God permits only those experiences that are for our good. If we are patient and let God work, we may be sure of a bright outcome. Because the future counts more than the present, let us endure whatever difficulties we may be called upon to bear. We can go through fire and water, knowing that God is in control and that He has a worthy purpose for everything.

"But you brought us to a place of abundance." Here is the end result of patiently enduring the fire and water. Here is the place to which God is leading us—a place of abundance. Thank God for such a prospect.

The Human Response in Worship

How do we respond to the experiences of life? Do we grumble and complain, or do we accept them as God's providences? Here is how the psalmist responds: *"I will come to your temple with burnt offerings and fulfil my vows to you"* (verse 13). The psalmist is speaking in terms of worship before the Christian era, when animal sacrifices pointed forward to Jesus, the Lamb of God. But we still assemble at a house of worship for mutual comfort and joy. We remember the words of the writer to the Hebrews: "Let us not give up meeting together, as some are in the habit of doing, but let us encourage one another—and all the more as you see the Day approaching" (Hebrews 10:25).

Are the vows we fulfill promises to serve God? Promises to pay a faithful tithe? Promises to help the church fulfill its worldwide mission of taking the gospel to all the world? The psalmist has special vows in mind, vows made in times of trouble: *"Vows my lips promised and my mouth spoke when I was in trouble"* (verse 14). Have we made promises that we find now difficult to keep? Did we, perchance, make them under duress? Did we say something like: "Lord, if You can get me out of this situation, I will . . ."? When God pulls us out of the embarrassing situation, we are relieved, but do we remember the promise we made? Honesty, reliability, and dependability are important character traits.

"I will sacrifice fat animals to you and an offering of rams; I will offer bulls and goats" (verse 15). The psalmist responds to God's generosity with his own generosity. What two people can afford to give may be very different. Someone has said that the size of the gift is determined by what is left in the purse. It is the spirit of the giver rather than the size of the gift that counts. Paul makes the following suggestion: "Each man should give what he has decided in his heart to give, not reluctantly or under compulsion, for God loves a cheerful giver" (2 Corinthians 9:7).

The Psalmist's Personal Testimony

"Come and listen, all you who fear God; let me tell you what he has done for me" (verse 16). In verse 5 the psalmist has already invited us to come and see. Now he asks us to come and listen! He has a personal testimony to give. Let us not hesitate to tell others of what God has done for us.

"I cried out to him with my mouth; his praise was on my tongue" (verse 17). The psalmist is telling us that at times he

felt that he had to be in touch with God. So he communicated with Him in loud prayer and praise.

"If I had cherished sin in my heart, the Lord would not have listened" (verse 18). The important principle here is that we cannot expect God to answer us or communicate with us if we persist in sin. One of the first things we should do is to confess our faults and ask God for forgiveness. Only then can we expect to be heard.

"But God has surely listened and heard my voice in prayer" (verse 19). Thank God for a prayer-hearing and a prayer-answering God! Have we not all had the precious experience of having prayers answered? We should all, like the psalmist, be praying and praising people, enjoying our daily communion with God.

Finally the psalmist concludes: *"Praise be to God, who has not rejected my prayer or withheld his love from me."* And we all respond, Amen and Amen!